MW01624919

DID NOT SEE THAT COMING

ACCOLADES

DID NOT SEE THAT COMING: Hope for the Single Parent *serves several purposes at once. It provides a lifeline to the overwhelmed single parent, struggling to make sense of a new reality. It guides you through the scary steps to regaining your balance. The friendly, comforting style makes you feel like you're talking to a sister or best friend. This is a must-read for all newly single parents--and even the not-so-newly single, too.*

Jennifer Harriman, KOMO News Radio

If you are a single parent just trying to get through another day, this is the book for you. Laurie tells her story and includes the stories of other single parents that will encourage and validate the struggles of going it alone. You will laugh, maybe cry, but most of all, you will see you are not alone in this journey.

Patrick Snow ~ author of *Creating Your Own Destiny*

This warm, personal book speaks to all women who are trying to do the best they can after the financial and emotional hit of divorce. Each person's experience is unique, but **DID NOT SEE THAT COMING: Hope for the Single Parent** *provides strategies and examples for getting past the myriad of commonalities for so many women living in the nearly impossible situation of single parenthood. Laurie Hardie uses her own story to comfort, inspire, and motivate others working their way toward good lives for themselves and their children. This is not another how-to manual; nor is it a check-off list of tasks for becoming perfect. It is a gentle guide for living, self-care, and forgiveness during a tough time that affects too many mothers.*

Heather Stark, MPA ~ author of
Why Doesn't She Just Leave? Real Women, Real Stories

Growing up and being raised by a single parent, I believe **DID NOT SEE THAT COMING** is *the guidance one needs to embrace their role as a single parent! My hat goes off to Laurie for writing a book with such rich content and one that can be used by single parents for years to come!*

Flora Morris Brown, Ph.D. ~ author of *Color Your Life Happy: Create the Success, Abundance, and Inner Joy You Deserve* Publishing Coach *www.ColorYourLifePublished.com*

DID NOT SEE THAT COMING *is many wonderful things for single parents: a reminder, a torch, a beacon, a boost, a balm, but most of all, a keepsake. For as we go after our dreams we will encounter bumps and sometimes potholes in the road. That's when Laurie's words will pull us forward, refuel our passion, and keep us moving toward the fulfilling lives we seek and deserve. Therefore, keep it nearby, because repeated readings are advised.*

Laymon A. Hicks ~ author of *A Treasure Chest of Motivation: 8 Jewels of Wisdom for a Young Adult's Success* and *Ignite Your Dreams: How to Build and Accelerate Your Life as a Top Notch Student* *www.LaymonHicks.com*

Did Not See That Coming *is an honest look at single parenting. A refreshing way to look at the, sometimes, heartbreaking struggles that are part of going it alone.*

BJ Farish ~ author of *Shattering Your Barriers*

"If you want to make God laugh, tell Him your plans." **DID NOT SEE THAT COMING** *teaches us that even in the midst of our most unimaginable circumstance, we can survive, thrive, live and even laugh.*

Kurt Eby ~ author of *Getting an A Without Trying*

DID NOT SEE THAT COMING *is a fresh and practical approach to what single parenting is all about. Laurie has truly done a great job in encouraging and coaching other single parents with strategies that work! Actually, this book is a must read for all parents!*

Ian S. Lavine, Th.B., Certified Behavioral Consultant

Even though I was the 'single parent' only on designated weekends and summer visitations, I look back and think how helpful it would have been back then to have had your book and your wisdom. Thanks in advance on behalf of those whom you will help.

Don Burrows ~ author of *Résumés That Resume Careers*

The next time you feel like you have nothing to give, no way to help, no one to support you, pick up **DID NOT SEE THAT COMING** *and receive a reminder that even when life is in a dark moment, there is always something, no matter how insignificant it may seem, to offer others.*

Randall Broad ~ author of *It's an Extraordinary Life – Don't Miss It*

DID NOT SEE THAT COMING *is a reminder that even when we think we have nothing to give, or no way to help, there is always something, no matter how insignificant it may seem, to offer others.*

Chris Bledy ~ author of *Beating Ovarian Cancer*

DID NOT SEE THAT COMING :

HOPE FOR THE SINGLE PARENT

by

Laurie Ann Hardie

Did Not See That Coming: Hope for the Single Parent

Address all inquiries to: www.DidNotSeeThatComing.com

Published by:

Aviva Publishing
Lake Placid, NY
518-523-1320

ISBN: 978-1-938686-33-7

For additional copies please visit:
www. DidNotSeeThatComing.com

Dedicated to

Jenna
Davis
&
Danen

ACKNOWLEDGMENTS

This book is about the support of community and connecting the dots to raise a family as a single parent. Thank you, Sue and Cheri, who know how to do the thrift with dignity. To my single mom posse - Cousin Donna, Crystal, Jennifer, Kim, and Gretchen, and those of you I have met along the way. To the Family Resource Center, Gail, Marilyn, and Amanda - you changed my life, believed in me, and let me give back. To my friends who saw me through some of my darkest hours - Precious, Laurie, Lori, Janine, Andy, Gail, Brenda, Sue, Cheri, Pam, Alice and Mike, Melissa, Charnell. Joy, thank you for finding humor in difficult situations to make me laugh. Thank you, Pastor Dick and Marilyn Jeffers, for modeling what it means to be a church in a community, reaching beyond the congregation.

This book would never have come to pass had I not made the connection with my publishing coach, Patrick Snow. Thank you for believing in my story and walking me through the process. Thank you for introducing me to a whole new community of friends through your work. Liam, what can I say? Editor extraordinaire, in the midst of so many things happening in your life, you continued to plug through making my ramblings into a story. Precious, thank you for picking up the final pieces and edits. Jennifer Harriman, your time and amazing editing/proofreading never cease to amaze me. Your bio tops all. You did what I could never do for myself. John and Angela, thanks for your support and eyes on this project. Emily, my amazing and talented niece, took on the cover and layout project. I love her words. "Auntie... Your title is ambitious so I wanted to tell your story in pictures." I love you and am so grateful for your wisdom and talent. To my friends who believe in me, in my story and continually cheer for me, I am blessed! Thank you for being on this incredible journey with me.

shop." Now, she speaks not only for her own company, but for motivational sales companies. She's having the time of her life.

I wish everyone could tune out the naysayers, but those negative voices are quite powerful. Most of us need the encouragement of someone who believes in us, but sometimes, even that isn't enough.

I had a client who wanted to write a novel. She had an excellent idea for a story, but something always got in the way. She chose to stop her coaching appointments with me, and I was sad that she let the negative "gremlins" talk her out of writing. I had to accept the fact that this wasn't her time. Still, it is never too late, and I hope she'll find her way.

There's a lot to be said for timing and life learning along the way. Sometimes we hear stories of people who achieve their dreams very quickly and think we should be able to get similar results. For me, it's been a struggle with many building steps along the way. I'm still learning to live in the moment and watch life unfold. I'm such an "anticipator" that I often can't wait for "what's next."

When I was a DJ, it was hard to wait for a song to finish, because I was so excited to play the next one! As a hopeless anticipator, I just want to get out, move on, or get to the dream, minus the journey. Looking back, I see the importance of the lessons offered.

At the time, though, I only saw them as diversions: a divorce that put my plans on hold, followed by a job with a scary boss who made working hours miserable. But I learned a computer program at that job that was essential for my "what's next."

I couldn't see the lessons then; I just wanted to be done. Finally, the anger and frustration from feeling stuck motivated me to revive my dream. Life is a journey, and we can fight it or embrace it.

Life is uncertain, and we can be frustrated or resentful – or, find a way to have faith and wonder how it will all play out I wish I would have embraced this concept sooner. It is amazing to me to begin to be okay with uncertainty. We can worry about the uncertainty of our lives, or we can choose to wonder. Worry has given me gray hair and indigestion. Wonder has given me hope and peace.

"Worry has given me gray hair and indigestion. Wonder has given me hope and peace. "

I would like to say that all of my clients have identified their dreams and are on their way. But the truth is that most of them are in process and some of them drop out or take a time out. We can all live with good enough. Some of us choose to stay there, and that's okay. In fact, it's better than just okay, because at least we have dreams. We have choices. When life gets in the way or we come up against obstacles, challenges, and dream crushers, we can say "Enough," or keep pushing on. Reviving the dream is not so much about "living the dream" as it is about discovering who you are, what you love, and what your purpose is. It's discovering or uncovering your greatness - what you were you created for. The question is, *"What has life given you to share, and in the process, how will you live at peace?"*

Embracing Our Quirkiness

Sometimes it seems like our dreams aren't useful because they're so quirky. By quirky, I mean something that seems peculiar or an idiosyncrasy that's hard to explain to other people.

My daughter, Jenna, is a horse trainer - or at least that's the closest description we have for what she does. She buys horses and works with them to get past issues, fears, or behavior problems. Sometimes she gets them when they're young and starts training them from the very beginning; other times she gets them at an older age. Seldom has she taken a horse from the beginning of its life to the end. She invariably sells them because she finds someone who suits that horse perfectly. And yet, she has always felt as though she somehow fell short because she hasn't taken horses through the complete cycle of training. Her way of training horses felt quirky.

When Jenna was younger, we went to visit Kim Meader's ranch. Kim is the author of *Bridge Called Hope: Stories from the Ranch of Rescued Dreams*. She rescues horses that have been neglected, abandoned, or abused. Once they're brought back to health, she matches them with kids: at-risk kids, foster kids, even kids with disabilities. We fell in love with her, the ranch, and her mission. We thought maybe this was what my daughter Jenna would do, too. After thinking it through, Jenna realized that the real inspiration was not to do the same thing Kim did, but that it was okay to specialize in training horses at certain crucial points in their lives.

Often times we feel as though our dream is quirky and can't put a name to it. It's ok. It may feel quirky and weird because it hasn't been labeled before, but that doesn't make it any less of a dream. It wasn't until many years later that my daughter discovered that she is not *just* a horse trainer, but an *interceptor*. She finds horses with behavior or trust issues that need a fresh start. She intercepts them and starts them down a new path. She can't explain why she's so good at it, or how she knows what horses to choose, but it works. She buys a horse, loves on it, spends time with it, builds up its trust, works through the issues, and then helps find its forever home. People can't believe the difference she makes in these horses – and the perfection of the matches she makes. She gets embarrassed, because she's just doing what comes naturally and is surprised when people are so touched by it. Before it had a name, she was unsure that her dream had any use in life. Now, she's found both the name, and the value.

We each have a purpose. For some, it's defined early on – seemingly inborn. For others, it comes as we navigate the maze of life. Sometimes, we spend our lives fighting a unique characteristic that turns out to be integral to our purpose.

I love the creative work of the author SARK, who wrote *Inspiration Sandwich*. In the book, she challenges each of her readers to embrace their *quirkiness*. Her quirk is to stay up all night - the time she works best. She sleeps during the day, and writes and draws in bed, in her pajamas, because that's what works *for her*.

What are your quirks?

What would it be like to talk with good friends about those quirks and embrace them, instead of trying to cover them up? Do you wonder what embracing your quirks would look like? All of my kids have a different quirk, and I've loved seeing how they've embraced them.

My daughter, like her cousin, loves wearing different socks, unmatched socks are her signature. Sometimes she feels like she doesn't quite fit in. Maybe that's why Jenna loves working with misfit horses and matching them with people who will love them.

My older son's quirk is that he has OCD (Obsessive-Compulsive Disorder). He's quite the perfectionist! He loves being a mechanic and he uses his perfectionism to make sure the job is done right. Everyone wants a mechanic like that!

My younger son is Bigger Than Life. When he comes into a room, he fills it with his appealing voice and his contagious humor. Sometimes I think he would make a great stand-up comedian. He was diagnosed with ADHD (Attention Deficit Hyperactivity Disorder), but he has found a way to manage it and make it work for him. He doesn't make it his identity, and he doesn't use it as an excuse. Now that he's out of school, he's discovering a whole new, wonderful world, because ADHD kids don't receive many kudos in the classroom.

Dream Weavings

Coming to terms with what makes us unique and sorting out the negative messages: What are your quirks? You might take time to acknowledge them by voicing them, writing them in your journal, or telling a friend. Can't see the value in your uniqueness? Set aside time to brainstorm with a friend about the possibilities s/he sees in your quirks.

Lots of people have useful quirks without even realizing it. Sometimes one comes by a talent so naturally that it doesn't seem like a gift, it just feels like who one is and what one does without thinking.

I spend a lot of time pointing out to my clients those things that come naturally for them could very well be part of their unique gifts. They struggle because it isn't spectacular; it's just what they do. I've seen hospitality, sewing, drawing, baking, gardening, listening, and a myriad of other talents. It's easy to take our gifts for granted and think that since it's easy for us, they don't matter because "anybody could do it."

Maybe you have a gift that goes hand in hand with who you are and what you do, but you aren't using it, or you're under so much pressure to use your talent that it seems more like a curse. Maybe you're already working toward your dream, but it isn't bringing you joy because you can't describe it in a way that others can understand, so it seems wrong. Maybe it seems so simple as to be silly.

My friend, Liam Atchison, says he sometimes has a hard time explaining to others what his calling in life is. Sometimes others spoil his sense of assurance when they wrinkle up their noses or shake their heads and ask "What is that?" He says that makes him question himself, like he must be nuts to be doing a job others can't understand. There's a great book by G.K. Chesterton called *The Club of Queer Trades,* describing a club where each member invented a new occupation previously unknown to humanity. It has brought him a great deal of comfort over the years.

How do you deal with the unexpected events that find their way into your life? Some people believe that misery is what God wants for their lives. For example, maybe you got pregnant before you planned, and now you feel you have to live with your "mistake" and never experience your dream. I wonder if that child could be in some way part of your "what's next"?

We often do this sort of thing, which I call letting my circumstances *name me* (have power over me). In the past, I've definitely let circumstances name me, rather than see the opportunities staring me in the face. I felt failure and shame. And it got in the way of my dream.

How about you? I wonder how miserable we have to be before we can believe God is really happy with our sacrifice? You don't have to change to do what you love. I say, just start living what you love. Life will happen whether we're doing what we love or not. Life happens, and when we're pursuing our purpose, we have more energy to deal with the difficult things in life. Think about your life, and if you dare, pull out a journal and write a short (or detailed, if you get into it) time line of your life. Start with the age of your earliest memory, and write one thing you remember.

Continue in this way until you arrive at your current age. Do you notice any themes emerging? Share your timeline with a friend, mentor, coach, counselor, or spiritual director to see if there are any untrue messages that you've latched onto. Some examples that could be etched in your memory would be:

"You are a burden."
"You're not important."
"You're not worth it."
"You're fat...ugly...untalented...talk too much."

How have those messages influenced your life in the past? How are they influencing you now? What might be some healing words to replace the negative, hurtful messages?

Negative Messages I Received

When I was a teen, my family members told me I was homely and needed to wear makeup. I would put it on at home, but as soon as I got to school, I ran to the bathroom to wash it off.

I hated the way I looked with the blues over my eyelids and the chunky black mascara. Invariably, at the next sink, another girl whose parents didn't allow her to wear makeup was putting it on!

For many years, I had this voice in my head from my home, telling me I was ugly, an idiot, and clumsy. Maybe the person who said it didn't even really mean it, but I still latched on and lived out the declaration of who I was TOLD I was.

Whenever I did something I felt stupid about, or saw myself in a mirror, I would repeat and reinforce those words, long after they were spoken by the original critic. In fact, I even added on to this monstrous monologue. I would do something like lock myself out of my car and the inner "mean girl" would say, "You're so stupid! Dummy. You always mess up."

"I began asking, 'What is the truth?'"

It was only when I started doing a timeline of my own life that I started identifying those messages and where they came from. Once I recognized what I was saying to myself, I began asking, "What is the truth?" The truth is, I locked myself out of my car. It's not stupid; in fact *smart* people do it all the time!

It's human nature, and it can be fun and funny, as well as frustrating! It can become an *adventure*, rather than a browbeating! It can become an *opportunity* to give others work, meet new people (like the locksmith) or give a friend a chance to give you a ride. See, if we can reframe those destructive messages and acknowledge the truth, we can then explore the opportunities presented.

Life happens, but it's how we deal with it that defines our paths. We waste opportunities to learn and grow by beating up on ourselves. Those who originally delivered the destructive messages are long gone, maybe even dead, but we keep the worst part of them alive by repeating their thoughtless cruelty.

I love the parable about a farmer whose horse ran off. All his neighbors and friends said, "Oh, how terrible!" But he said, "Maybe it is, and maybe it isn't." When the horse came back and brought other wild horses with it, friends and neighbors said, "That's wonderful!" The farmer said, "Maybe it is, and maybe it isn't." His son fell and broke his leg while trying to "break" the wild horses. Friends and neighbors said, "That's terrible." The farmer said, "Maybe it is, maybe it isn't." Then the military draft was put into effect and his son wasn't able to go because his leg was broken.

My friend and associate life coach, Suzette, and I were at a middle school girls' empowerment camp, talking about facing fears. A darling young lady spoke up and said she really wanted to sky dive, but she was a little afraid. She told the story she read in a magazine about a woman who was sky diving and when she pulled the chute, there wasn't one in the pack. The girl told us the woman fell to the ground and landed on an ant hill. It turns out, the woman broke a lot of bones, but doctors said she lived because the ants biting her kept her heart going! We hear stories like this all the time, where something that seems so bad, turns out okay. Maybe it is good, maybe it isn't.

"Life happens, but it's how we deal with it that defines our paths."

What would it be like to see your life as a movie with you as the main character? You don't know what happens next, but you're fully engaged in the movie/life. Is this the part where she (meaning you, the main character) will meet someone who really impacts her life? Or will she discover something that seems like a big mistake on her part, is really a "blessing in disguise?" The audience knows what happens to her isn't because she's "dumb, clumsy, ugly, or worthless." The audience knows *this is what has to happen* to get to the resolution of the story—the happy ending or the moment of fulfillment.

What if you're right where you are supposed to be, but you're so busy feeling like a failure that you miss the opportunity you didn't see coming? What if this is the way your life is *supposed* to play out? We can't determine the future, but we can pursue what we love and wonder what doors will open and who we will meet along the way.

"What if this is the way your life is supposed to play out?

Don't mistake this for "everything is going to be okay" because it isn't. Life is tough and difficult things are going to happen, whether you're doing what you love or not. Tough times don't mean you're off track or making a mistake. Tough times are not a sign to give up your dream. Tough times are life. The Bible tells us there will be tough times for the ones who ultimately overcome.

Life is uncertain, but I can almost guarantee that you will have trials and struggles, especially if you want to make a difference. A friend's father-in-law had a plaque on his desk that read, "To avoid criticism: Say nothing, do nothing, be nothing." The same could be said for those who want to avoid suffering. Trials don't name you.

I don't want to be that lady who married the gay man. I don't want to be that mom whose child got in trouble. I don't want to be that person who can't pay bills and is losing a house because of a tough economy. These things are not who we are; these things are the stuff of life and what happens. *Who we are is who we are, regardless of our circumstances.*

Just Wondering:

What are your quirks?

What do you do that's as natural as breathing? You may need to have others who are close to you identify these things if you aren't able to see clearly.

Is there some aspect of your gift you haven't been able to accept, or even seen as a detriment?

Is there something that made you feel shame or bitterness, causing you to make a negative life rule? Example: I will *never* ________?

Is there a message that caused you to close up? Give up? Is there something getting in the way of doing what you love because it has become a barrier? Like math and nursing? What have you been told you're not good at?

Have you ever heard, been told, "You'll never measure up," or words to that effect?

What "life messages" are getting in the way?

What has named you? For instance, "I'm such a klutz"?

"Who we are is who we are, regardless of our circumstances."

I'm convinced that almost no group of people struggles more with these questions than single parents. In the coming chapters, I want you to join me in a stroll with other single parents who have struggled, and yet found ways to identify and remember their dreams, and not let divorce or being single name them.

This is a journey. We're in this together, and the more we take off our masks and share our true selves, the more amazing things happen. Rather than being judged, we begin to be embraced. Not always, but you already know that. See, people would rather hear from fellow strugglers than someone who has it all figured out and seems flawless. (I know I would!)

Come along and meet my friends and sojourners in this event called life. This is a journey to encourage and inspire you to keep up the good work, hang in there, and most of all, never give up your dreams.

My hope is that the stories shared in this book will remind you that you're not alone. Many are traveling the same path as you. Maybe in a different way or by a different vehicle - but no matter whether we travel by car, bike, horse, wheelchair, or on foot, we all have breakdowns, run out of gas, and experience other setbacks.

The point is: We don't have to do it alone. So I'm thinking, maybe if I share my stories and my friends tell theirs, you will tell yours. Thank you for picking up this book. Grab a cup of coffee or tea and enjoy the friendship. Oh, and grab your journal too - because you just might be inspired to write.

2

And They Lived Happily Ever After for Awhile

"Destiny is a mysterious thing, sometimes enfolding a miracle in a leaky basket of catastrophe." - *Francisco Goldman*

Have you ever gotten a telephone call that changed your life? Mine came in the afternoon from one of my best friends. She had just gotten a hair cut from her favorite hairdresser, my husband. She asked if I knew what he was "up to," and I assumed she was talking about my husband's new lifestyle.

I knew he had been behaving differently, but I didn't know what to do about it. I admitted to her that I thought he was gay, and that I believed he wanted to be "caught" so he wouldn't have to tell me. Never before had I revealed these secret thoughts -not even to my sister.

It was huge to hear myself voicing these suspicions to another human being. From that very moment, everything seemed to run together until the day he left.

One night, he came home extremely late, so I asked him to spend the night somewhere else. Apparently, that was the opportunity he was looking for. He gathered up his stuff, and practically cartwheeled out the door. He thought he was finally free.

Plenty of other people have similar stories. Not necessarily that their spouses are gay, but their spouse wanted out of the marriage and just didn't have the courage to end it. So instead, the one who wanted to leave did everything they could to make their remaining spouse the "bad guy"—that is, the one who had to draw the line and ultimately end it.

I remember one of my best friends, who lived nearby, saying she was confused when I seemed upset about the separation and imminent divorce. She asked, "Laurie, isn't this what you wanted?" My answer was no, and yes. The truth was, I knew our marriage was on the rocks, but I was terrified to be on my own. How would I survive, make a living, and raise three kids? The marriage really ended years ago. But we limped along and raised three children together. You know what I really wanted? I wanted him to love me and *not* be gay.

At this time I was also struggling with depression, and this sent me spiraling downward. My physician helped me get on track with anti-depressants by adding a prescription to what I was already taking. Unfortunately, I only felt worse, and the doctor changed my prescription again. Anti-depressants can be a blessing to a non-functioning brain, but if they're not right, it can get very ugly, very quickly.

I decided I had to be proactive to make sure I was doing okay, even if it meant changing medicines, which was emotionally risky, physically taxing, and time consuming. It was tough, but I did it for my kids' sake. All I really felt like doing was going to the liquor store and buying the hardest stuff there, whatever that was. Given the long history of alcoholism in my family, I nixed that idea. The last thing I needed was another problem I'd have to deal with later.

My mom ingrained in me how important it was to look great all the time, especially when you were married, so your husband wouldn't leave you. From the time I was 11 years old, I would get up early every day to make sure I had my makeup on before anyone else was awake. And here I was, in my forties, with a husband who had left me. Did I not look great enough?

Now, first thing in the morning, I would walk the kids and the dog to the school bus stop in my sweats, with wild hair and no makeup. After the kids were on their way, I would go home and cry my eyes out. I felt so lost, confused, and I didn't know what to do despite the fact that I was a life coach. "*A LIFE COACH!!!*"_I thought, "And I just can't coach myself through this one. How will I make a living? How will I survive? What am I supposed to tell our kids?" This wasn't my life plan! It was my worst fear! Plus, I discovered I was right all along - my husband didn't love me. He just couldn't.

"Taking off the ring was so difficult."

The morning after he left, I called a friend who had told me her story about being abandoned by her husband. She and her two daughters ended up homeless, forced to live in a shelter. She didn't feel safe because of drug deals going on in the building, and it was hell on earth for her. She survived, and eventually met her new husband and has been married ever since.

Remembering her story gave me courage. I thought, if she could make it, then so could I. I was trying to make sense of it all when she told me I would be okay, and to remember, "*It is what it is.*"

Taking off the ring was so difficult. It made me feel so vulnerable and alone. When I was with my kids and had no ring on my finger, it seemed to scream, "LOOK! She's NOT MARRIED!" I felt like a pathetic loser. A failure. Alone. I felt like everyone noticed that I no longer wore a wedding ring, and that somehow made me bad.

Shortly after he left, my husband dealt a blow that felt like it was just too much to bear. While stopping by to pick up some of his things, he told me that he'd had several AIDS tests - and added that he never loved me. He said he just married me to prove to his dad he wasn't gay.

This conversation took place thirteen years and three kids after our wedding. In those days, AIDS tests took seven years to determine whether or not one had been infected. I'll never forget year number seven after he left when I finally knew for sure I didn't have AIDS.

After he told me he never loved me, I was so stunned, so crushed, so absolutely humiliated that I just couldn't quit crying. I still didn't want the kids to see how sad I was, so when they would get home from school, I did my best to act upbeat.

There inevitably came the point, though, when I couldn't keep up the façade and my youngest, who was six years old, caught me crying. He brought me a bath towel, and dried my tears. *It had to be a bath towel;* it was a lot of tears. He's always seen the bigger picture. Those weren't just tears; that was a river of grief. Thank you, Danen.

"She never offered advice or a quick fix."

When I put my kids to bed that night, my friend Gail called. When I answered the phone, I told her I couldn't talk because I was crying. She came over right away. We drank tea, and she listened while I relayed the conversation with the kids' dad from earlier. She was with me when there were no words to say. She *never* offered advice or a quick fix. She validated me, listened, and cried. I was heard. Somehow, I could make it through another day.

This reminded me of a time when my friend Cheri called. She was so upset about something and, silly me, I thought she wanted *advice.* Fortunately, I had laryngitis and I couldn't talk. So I listened and hemmed and hawed a lot. When the conversation was over, I felt horrible because I wasn't able to advise or encourage her.

She called back the next day to say, "Laurie, thank you for listening last night, I felt so understood and thank you for *not* trying to fix me." It turns out, laryngitis can be a gift. Now, I'm learning to listen well.

"The outside world often imposes a time frame for those who grieve."

After separating from my husband, I kept trying to cheer myself up, but nothing was working. I did everything I knew: working home based jobs, reading my Bible every day for peace and courage, going out in public despite the questions and pitiful looks. Friends and acquaintances were sympathetic and helpful in so many amazing ways that I don't know how we could have made it without them.

Casseroles showed up on our porch, money was slipped under the door in an envelope, and cards with wonderful sentiments arrived by snail mail. Despite doing what seemed like all the right things and having many tangible blessings offered to me, I still couldn't get over the depression.

I just felt like a failure and figured I should have done more: worked harder, prayed more, and acted more wisely. I felt embarrassed for being fooled, and shame for this assault on my femininity. I felt heartbroken for not being able to help my children more.

I knew I couldn't hold on to our apartment much longer with my income, and I didn't know what to do. My friend, Precious, called daily to check in, and I kept telling her I felt I should be feeling better and moving on, but I was sad and confused and still too embarrassed to spend much time in public places.

It wasn't the same for my ex, though. Once it was all "out in the open," he was on with his new life, new boyfriend, and new home with a stunning vista. The kids and I were stuck in an apartment behind the hair salon he worked in, with a view of big garbage dumpsters. Precious said, "But of course you're sad and confused!" This was music to my ears. I had permission!

The outside world often imposes a time frame for those who grieve. It gives them six months to be sad and upset, but then they need to buck up and move on. Whether it is a divorce, death, break-up, or illness, friends and relatives will be able to show sympathy for about half a year. Then they let you know you should be doing better by now. *But of course.* Those words carried me through years of interesting circumstances.

When the kids' dad filed for divorce, I was the one who had to break the news. I told them this separation was going to be permanent. Dad and I are divorcing. My middle child piped up and asked, "Does this mean we will have two moms and two dads like our friends?" My response? "I'm pretty sure I'll always be your *only* mom." *But of course.*

Where Would I Be Without Friends

That was a pretty significant declaration. Now I was committed, but we needed other people. I don't know where the kids and I would be without our friends. Our first Christmas after the separation was fast approaching. I was just going through the motions, but I knew I needed to decorate for the holidays. "Are you kidding?" I asked myself. I didn't want to decorate, but I got a tree on sale two days before Christmas Day. I pulled the decorations out of storage, including the nativity with green magic marker across baby Jesus' face. (As a baby, my youngest discovered felt tip markers. Joseph had a nice big black mustache—mutton chop sideburns, too.)

At the grocery store, I ran into an acquaintance who said she had heard about my situation – and slipped me a fifty dollar bill. I was shocked and humbled. The next day, she called and asked if she and her husband could put up Christmas lights on our house. I said, "Thanks, but I don't have any." "No worries," she said. The next day, Sue and Rick brought lights and a ladder and put up an awesome display.

When the kids got home from school, they were so surprised and pleased. We made it through our first holiday on our own. And get this: after Christmas, Rick and Sue came back and took all the decorations down! "I can't do this on my own, Lord!" *But of course*

Even though I had always considered myself a morning person, mornings now became the hardest part of the day. Getting kids up and walking them to the bus stop felt as difficult as running a marathon.

There were two other moms at the bus stop, and they were always dressed and ready for the day. I didn't know them, and I was repeatedly embarrassed about my appearance, but I just didn't have enough energy to pull it together.

Gradually, we began chatting a little each day at the bus stop, and I really grew to love these mothers. They seemed so together and fun and smart, and they liked me and didn't judge me for looking like a wreck. One day, my story spilled out, and they were so kind. We started having lunch together every few months and they became a lifeline, a connection that said I was okay—still a member of the human race, in good standing! Their friendship assured me I would be fine. I could still make friends even at my worst. There were others, too. I was making friends that I wouldn't have even known otherwise. I'm so grateful to the pharmacist, and the school principal, Kathy, for seeing more than just a sad, dowdy woman in sweats.

They forgave me for having the dog that peed on one of their kid's shoes. They didn't seem to be shocked that I didn't wear make-up. They listened to my tragic tale without demanding that I buck up. They saw me, warts and all, and still accepted me into their circle and made me feel that I was okay. They treated me like a friend, despite the fact that they had seen me at my very worst.

Next, I was ready to move my ex-husband's things out. He was a "collector," so there were boxes and boxes and boxes and more boxes of clothes and shoes. My college roommate and best friend, Joy, came over to help me with this overwhelming project.

I was in a state of numbness, but Joy made it fun. Joy liked to shake things up a bit, so we may have accidentally spilled our coffee in some shoes. Oops! Or … a shirt or two may have ended up with a hole or missing sleeve or button. I'm just saying accidents happen. We laughed and cried and drank coffee and ate chocolate-malted Easter egg candy.

I was getting ready to move out of the apartment into a camper.
It was a difficult time, to say the least. I had to get rid of everything possible and only store what was absolutely necessary. The animals went into foster care. This time, friends Sue and Pam came to help me clean. We cranked up the country music, and I'm sure we

got high on the fumes from bleach, ammonia, and oven cleaner. We didn't have a mop, but that didn't stop us - we got very creative. We scrubbed and laughed, and that made it fun, memorable, and hysterical. I cherish those rare moments of gut-wrenching laughter.

"I don't know what I would have done without my many types of friends."

There's an email that makes the rounds over and over again that you may have seen. It speaks of friends and the amount of time each one spends in your life. Someone may be your friend for a day, a year, or a lifetime. But the significance of each encounter and each relationship puts an indelible mark on our lives. I don't know what I would have done without my many *types* of friends.

They were all so different from each other, but the mosaic of their influence in my life was just what I needed. They were my lifeline. Each had something wonderful to offer. They were all so *there* for me, that I felt like I was taking but not giving much back. I know, I know. They're such great friends that they would tell me I was dead wrong about not offering them anything in return. Still, they inspired me so much, I want to spend the rest of my life giving something back.

Now I can lend a listening ear, give compassion, and offer friendship. It reminds me of this great poem, posted on the wall in the pediatrician's office, about a messy house with fingerprints on the walls. The point of the poem is that relationships are more important than a clean house. For too long, I held many friends at bay at my doorstop because I was ashamed of the condition of my house. In fact, in the *Messies Anonymous* books, they mention that people who are very relational tend to be even messier because their priorities are people, versus household tasks. Makes sense!

Despite all the help and encouragement the realization hit: I am single, with three kids, and forty, on my way to living in a camper. My friends found ways to keep my spirits up. No anedotes, no advice, no "shoulds": they just offered a listening ear, a helping hand, support, and laughter. But most of all, my friends believed in me even when I couldn't.

If I could, I would make an honor roll of all those friends. I will never forget who they were, and are, in my life. God showed up in my life through people who gave without thought of return.

So how many times had I missed God showing up because my gaze was down? My eyes were so averted because of my tragedy that I didn't recognize all the divine encounters that were taking place in and around me. Finally, the wonderful day came when I said, "Enough of that already!" I prayed that I would recognize the tastes of heaven that could only be attributed to God. I wanted to be more ready—more available to people along the way.

Now, if I feel a nudge to talk to a stranger I usually act on it. I ride the bus to work, and there have been many occasions when I really just wanted to read my book, but I felt a nudge to talk to the person next to me. Usually, I'm so blessed by the conversations and just plain amazed by what I see.

Once I watched a girl in a seat facing me change her clothes without showing any flesh! When she was finished, she pulled a small cake out from under her coat and frosted it just in time for her stop. No kidding. A cake! Was it a quick-change artist or an angel?

I met other, less outrageous people. There was Luke, a male model, and Elizabeth, visiting from Kenya. And there was pain and hardship and triumph, too: I spoke with a lady who left an abusive husband. There was an older woman who started taking dancing lessons again after caring for a sick husband for years. She said she was getting her life back through dancing. There was a woman whose grief over her mother's sudden death had kept her from celebrating holidays, but maybe next year she will try. Maybe Thanksgiving, she said.

"...everyone is drawn in when encouragement is afoot!"

A single mom on her way to traffic court told me she cleaned houses to support her girls. I asked her what she would do if she could do anything. She whispered, "Be a model, but I'm too old." I asked what she loved about modeling, and she said it was fashion—she loved clothes. So we talked about her love of clothes. I encouraged her to hold on to her dream.

When she asked what I did and I told her that I was a traffic reporter on the radio, the homeless man who I thought was asleep next to us piped up and said, "Hey, I listen to you all the time!" See, everyone is drawn in when encouragement is afoot!

Get this: My bus friends and I started the "510 Book Club" on the express bus to downtown Seattle. A few of us started talking about books we read and liked. Pretty soon, we were deciding on a book we could all read and then talk about during our bus ride each day. Then there was the community college math teacher on his way to the VA hospital. We were having a nice visit, until he started making me do math! Seriously, I got off the bus early. I know I've missed divine moments in my selfishness, but I'm so grateful for the ones I paid attention to. It's all part of the adventure.

I began to draw soul breaths from these encounters. And because I was available, I'm sure I became the divine encounter for others!

I made it through the initiation into single parenthood because of good friends, a wonderful family, and a wonderful community. I made it because people stood by me, validated me, and believed in me. I like to think I have a strong faith in God, but during such a difficult time, I was blessed with the hands and feet of God disguised as those who were surrounding me.

Just Wondering:
Have you had a divine encounter? What was it like? Have you had a friend or friends step in to make your tough time easier? Write about it in your journal or tell someone about it or even reminisce with that friend. What did you take away from the experience?

When I look back to write about my experience, I am even more grateful for friends now than I was at the time, because I was so caught up in my own grief. What friend reflections do you see more clearly in retrospect? What is your favorite friend-helping-out story? Have you reminded them lately about it and how much it meant to you?

As a coach, encourager, and friend, often the only thing I had to give back was my memories of the tough times and how each friend saw me through. It is a gift to reflect that back to our friends, even years after an event. Think about or make a list of some friend memories you would like to revisit.

3

The Tale You've Fallen Into

"I wonder what sort of tale we've fallen into?"
- Sam: Fellowship of the Rings by J.R.R. Tolkien

"Yes, that's so," said Sam. "And we shouldn't be here at all, if we'd known more about it before we started but I suppose it's often that way. The brave things in the old tales and songs Mr. Frodo: adventures, as I used to call them. I used to think that they were things the wonderful folk of the stories went out and looked for, because they wanted them, because they were exciting and life was a bit dull, a kind of sport, as you might say. But that's not the way of it with the tales that really mattered. Or the ones that stay in the mind. Folk seem to have been just landed in them, usually their paths were laid that way, as you put it." [1]

Sometimes we think that adventures are things that happen to other people, not us. So when we're thrust into new experiences, we often clamber to get back to what seems like normalcy, rather than employing curiosity to "take a look around" at our new surroundings.

I would love to have the perspective of Samwise Gamgee. He didn't ask for a rambling life, and had literally moments to steel himself for his journey into the unknown. Nevertheless, this humble son of a gardener, who had never before wandered more

[1]J. R. R. Tolkien, *The Lord of the Rings*. Single-volume Edition (Boston: Houghton Mifflin, 1999), p. 696.

than a few miles from his home, had the good sense to recognize a new chapter—or entirely new tale—of his life in the midst of its unfolding. Sam embraced this newness and turned all of his acquired wisdom to ask questions and navigate unknown territory.

The "adventure" of a person who is suddenly a single parent is no less daunting in many ways than Sam's. So how does a single parent accept -- no, embrace -- the adventure and choose to live fully, rather than just survive?

My sister is a schoolteacher who loves children's literature, and she has taught me much about the characters we've all grown to love. We've discussed James in *James and the Giant Peach*, *Cinderella*, *Snow White*, and *Harry Potter*, and it's astounding what all these characters have in common.

These children were abandoned and taken in by cruel family members, and despite being treated badly, their goodness survives the abuse. These are our heroes.

When I get to know people of character who have survived incredibly difficult childhoods, it reminds me that good does indeed overcome evil. Not only are there good kids with *terrible* parents, but there are terrible children with *remarkable* parents. There doesn't seem to be any rhyme or reason in how our kids turn out, because there are no guarantees.

Just as it's hopeful that abusive parents won't prevent children from transcending their childhoods and living as loving, giving adults, so it's hopeful that diligent parents will have responsible kids.

I have friends who have adopted children with disorders that have made their lives *extremely* difficult. Yet they give these children loving homes and stability and do their best while they endure being misunderstood, and even blamed, for their bad behavior. It's so easy to blame the parents, but the behavior of some of these kids lines up exactly with their disorders.

"Don't use your children to hurt your spouse..."

In the state of Washington, parents who divorce are required to take a parenting class. I took it. It was a great learning experience and it focused on the kids. Some of the advice I gleaned: Don't use your children to hurt your spouse, and don't keep them from their other parent, even if your ex doesn't pay child support.

If I were pressed to summarize the big idea of the class, it would be to put the kids first, and don't put your "stuff" on them or use them to deliver messages to your ex. Though I enjoyed my classmates, it made me sad to meet women who had been stay-home moms, but were now forced into the workplace. No matter what, the kids' lives were turned upside down.

Dad leaves, mom goes to work, they have to move, and sometimes change schools. Children's lives are disrupted, and they don't have any say in what is happening. I tried to make any decisions concerning my children with this in mind. The instructor pointed out that kids may blame themselves or question their parents' love for them.

They don't want to choose between mom and dad. This played a huge role in my decision to not go to work right away and leave them with a babysitter. Because of my choice, we ended up living in a camper trailer at a local campground. It turns out, living in a camper was great fun for young boys, but devastating for a twelve-year-old girl.

I went back and forth between thinking, "I'm forty with three kids, living in a camper," and feeling like a failure and "I'm on staff at a campground! What a dream come true!" It was a new kind of normal. Life as my kids and I knew it would never be the same again.

It was depressing to focus on the negative, but when I focused on the possibilities, I could find peace. It was a constant battle trying to live in the positive. I had to make myself "enjoy" the day, because thinking about the future and all of the uncertainties made my head spin.

My kids are marvelous and resilient and I'm so proud of them - but I expect they'll have to deal with certain childhood issues as they grow older. I'll support their processes and own up to my contributions to their struggles. Still, I look back and see that I was trying to ease their pain in as many ways as I knew how.

One time there was a job I wanted to take in another state – but my kids didn't want to move away from their dad, so I turned it down. I also chose not to date again after a very short-lived second marriage. I decided the kids had been through enough, and I didn't want them to have to deal with a mom dating, falling in love, and getting her heart broken again and again. For me, that was the best choice I could make for my family.

When our camping adventure was over, I found a ranch where I could work and we could live. It looked like the owner wanted someone to take care of the horses and the rest of the place, in exchange for reduced rent. It seemed ideal: the fifty-five acre tract was close to the kids' schools and offered plenty of room for my boys to wander. We kept my daughter's horse, (I just couldn't bear to take that away, too.) and there was plenty of room for her, too. I didn't have another job, and I couldn't afford full rent.

However, when the landlord found out what my real situation was, he said he didn't want a single mom to rent the farm. We were devastated. Jenna and I cried and cried in our disappointment. The idea that I could rent a place like that with no job or means of income was ridiculous. What was I thinking?

"Go ahead and risk being disappointed..."

Well, two days later the landlord called and said, "Come and see the house." I said, "Hey, I'm the single mom you said you didn't want!" He paused, and then said, "I know, but everyone around here keeps telling me you're the one I need to rent this place."

The kids and I fell instantly in love with the ranch, and we experienced a blessed reunion. Jenna's horse was finally with us. We got our dog out of foster care, and it seems a dusty kitty had bonded with our dog, Bear, so she came along, too.

This became my place of healing. There were gardens with flowers, and raspberries, fruit trees, horses and even a special chicken! Snowy was the coolest fluffy white chicken. Danen caught her at a barnyard scramble, and she lived in a kitty carrier on our front porch. Our big dog, Bear, and Snowy became the best of friends. We were a family again, and we were going to be okay.

I can't remember all the details of how rent and things worked out, but I had help from friends, and I was able to secure a type of HUD (housing) financing that supplemented my rent. Sometimes things that seemed so impossible just worked out with neither rhyme nor reason, but good things happened.

Though I've stepped into many situations by faith, they don't all work out as beautifully as this one did. But every one of them has been an adventure, and I'm glad for what I learned. I hear people tell me about their dreams, and they will say, "I don't want to get my hopes up." So I say. "Aww…get your hopes up!" They say, "I don't want to be disappointed." But I remind them, "Go ahead and risk being disappointed, it won't kill you."

Disappointment may make you feel as if your heart is breaking, but it's all part of the voyage. When life hands you crap, you have to live through it. I'm not saying it's easy, but when times get tough and our hearts get broken, we tell ourselves too quickly we're never going to do that again. That's just self-protection, and if we resolve to never be hurt again, we're in danger of making safety our highest priority. What kind of way is that to live? We end up in isolation, not trusting anybody else, and never experiencing anything remarkable.

I challenge you to live the adventure. Wonder what comes next. Find an adventure like *The Lord of the Rings* or C.S Lewis' *Chronicles of Narnia* and read it to yourself and to your kids. Some people call those books fantasy, but the characters live with loyalty, courage, and passion, and that sure seems like the way we ought to live in the "real" world. *Why not* begin to see life as an adventure? What if we could wonder what's next instead of hoping for one ultimate ending we control? Live in the journey.

Okay, so sure, I'm looking back as I say this. I came up against huge challenges and things that seemed impossible - but when I chose to believe it was all part of the adventure and that somehow, some way, we would get through it, I had the sensed of being part of something bigger than myself. There were times when I would be in bed, and I would let that little thought of "I can't do this, I'm not going to make it" sneak in. That's when I couldn't let it just be about me. I told myself, over and over, "Somehow, some way, we are going to make it, *we have to*," and that kept me going.

It was logical to think I wasn't going to make it. Even with one breadwinner working full time in this economy, it's often not enough to raise a family. Community, friends, family, faith, and believing in the adventure, the "what's next" all kept me going. It is there for each of us, though it may be hard to recognize at first.

Help may arrive in a form that seems unfamiliar. I prayed my eyes would be open to see the adventure through all my worry and neediness. When I was first told that someone in my church had a camper that the kids and I could live in for awhile, I'm pretty sure that in my ingratitude, I thought, "There's no way I'll ever live in a camper!" But it didn't take long to run out of options, and what seemed like certain death became the adventure of a lifetime. I'm deeply thankful for that wonderful camper now. Go figure.

"...there was no defending, or blaming, just validating."

Early on, I learned not to talk bad about the kids' dad to them or in front of them. The times when I slipped, I could see it hurt them, so I stopped. Once I was frustrated and venting to a friend when I thought the kids were asleep, but one of them overheard and corrected me the next morning. The ex is still their parent. I tried to find what good I could, what truth I could, and focused on that. I bit my tongue a lot. But I validated the kids. When they were frustrated or disappointed with dad, I would say, "That must be hard," or "I can see you're really ticked off." But there was no defending, or blaming, just validating.

Giving validation without getting all puffed up thinking I was the better parent for the moment was tough. I knew that if I used their frustration as an opportunity to get on my soapbox and say everything I thought was wrong with their dad, it would only backfire. I wanted my experience to be believed – I wanted validation for myself - but still had to control my tongue. I knew that in a few days they would be over it, but I would have really blown it in their eyes had I joined in the venting.

Some friends who knew the real story would see my restraint and call me a saint. As much as I like being called a saint, the truth is, I was just surviving. I wanted a relationship with my kids more than I wanted to prove how much I'd been betrayed and hurt. In the end, I know my kids are grateful that my ex and I can get along and the whole family can be together for graduations and weddings.

I've heard women who talk about their ex in front of their kids, and when I mention it to them, they say they don't really care, or insist the children are too young to understand. I've even heard women talk about the kids' dad in a detrimental way while still married to the guy. Don't do this to your kids!

Kids know more of what you're talking about than you think. Kids are smart. They read between the lines. I know what it is like to be hurting, angry or sad. I know how hard it is to find time away from the kids in order to safely vent, but it's so worth it to find a way.

When you were a child, did your parents talk about each other to you? Did they fight in front of you? What did it feel like?

Here's the deal. You have complete permission to vent and yell. Break dishes. Throw anything you want, out of range of children, of course. Do it with friends, have a party, get it out, but do it on your time. This is good policy for frustrated grandparents, too. Don't badmouth the kids' parent, even the prodigal one.

As my adventure continued, my greatest fear just had to be realized. My daughter went to live with her dad. It just so happened to also be the best thing for her at the time, as well as the boys and me. It gave us the freedom to make a move we had been too paralyzed to make. But I couldn't stop crying! I was heartbroken! I missed her every day, even though she was only about a mile down the road. It was supposed to be temporary, but it hurt like crazy.

Her dad had different rules, and it was so difficult for me to let go. I was often tempted to threaten, boss, and cajole her from afar, and to try to get her dad more involved in my agenda. The illusion of control is just that, an illusion. Her dad and I have different belief systems, and in the end, Jenna had to choose what she believes. I had to let her live her own story. I had to let go, and trust the work I did as a parent in the early years was enough to get her through with no guarantees.

"The illusion of control is just that, an illusion."

That said, I still tried to guilt my poor daughter into coming home. I didn't think she or I would survive her living anywhere but with me. I did survive, and so did she.

I'm so grateful for my friend Wendy, who was divorced and remarried. She also had a daughter who went to live with her dad. We had lunch together once a week for the next three or four years. We reminded each other to choose what was more important: being right, or having a relationship with our girls.

Many times I wanted to try to force the issue and get my daughter to move back. I would write her long letters before reconsidering and ripping them up. Then I would write a long letter to her dad and tear *that* up. But Wendy's humor and gentle support would bring me back to reality.

The truth was that our daughters were living with their fathers, and it wasn't the end of the world. It was something they needed, and it was a way they could have some choice in their lives. No matter what, we so love our kids that when they move out, we feel like we failed them, and that's difficult to deal with.

When my daughter decided not to come back home, I happened to be attending a Women of Faith conference in Oregon. I was crying a lot more than I was listening to the speakers, and the lady sitting next to me started talking with me at the break. She told me that her daughter had moved out and was living with her dad -- and that it was the best thing for her daughter.

She spoke about how hard it was, but that time with her dad was something she really needed. After throwing a fit, she realized she had to let go. Somehow, this made me feel better, though my feeling like a failure was about me and didn't accomplish anything for my daughter. I'm not saying I didn't mess up, but I began to trust that this was the right thing.

I'm happy to say that today my daughter is a grown woman, married, and we have a wonderful relationship. My biggest fear was that she would grow up, not want to be around me, or have anything to do with me. It didn't happen, and I'm so grateful. I wonder, if I could have let go of that fear, or recognized it earlier, if we would have escaped some of that energy-sapping drama. It was fear, more than love, that made trying to control my daughter more appealing.

What felt like control was just an illusion, masquerading as control. The hardest challenge was admitting I couldn't make anyone else do my bidding. Once I started thinking about this and putting my coaching skills into action, I was able to learn some valuable lessons from my kids.

For example, they would see movies I didn't approve of when they were with their dad. So we would have discussions about the movie. What did you like? What did it mean? I tried to not get defensive (difficult!) But this allowed me to learn what they were thinking and what was influencing them.

I asked questions to make them think and challenge their values and really think about who they wanted to be. When the kids' dad took them to the Gay Pride Parade, now called Pride Parade, in Seattle, with his partner, we had a lively discussion.

Every now and then, it was tempting to use my hurt heart to try to turn them against him, but really, I loved it that they could accept him for who he was.

Their friends would ask questions like, "Who's that guy with your dad all the time?" and my kids would say, "It's his boyfriend," and I would breathe a sigh of relief when the other kid would just say, "Oh. Cool." It was tremendous pressure to feel responsible for what their friends said.

There were other overwhelming pressures as well. Video games became a sore spot. My boys loved them, but we started hearing news reports of kids overdoing it and acting out violently. We heard video games linked to the Columbine, Colorado disaster of 1998. This was daunting for a single parent. We can only monitor so much, after all!

I ended up turning the living room into the video game room, because that way, I could be in the kitchen and hear what was going on. When kids are wrapped up in what they're doing, they forget mom or dad is nearby. I couldn't keep them from playing video games, but I could somewhat monitor the ratings.

At their dad's house, however, they were allowed to play whatever they wanted. Timidly, I would ask about the reality of the game experience, and they thought my questions were ridiculous. They seemed to get that just because they could drive a hot car on a video game, that didn't mean they could just get in a car and drive. I'm not making light of video games. Too much fantasy can rob families of relational time. I'm just highlighting my fears about how responsible I felt for my kids' choices.

"Too much fantasy can rob families of relational time."

I worked very hard at keeping them busy, even by living on a farm and giving them outside places to enjoy. I tried to put a limit on "too much," but there is a limit to what limits can accomplish. Bottom line: Try as I might, I could not control any of those who were closest to me.

In his last year of high school, my youngest son also went to live with his dad. That's the way things worked out. It wasn't what I wanted, but with divorce things are rarely the way you want them. It's a school for learning that one cannot control others. I'm learning to let go of the illusion of control. It's futile to attempt to impose my agenda to guarantee my life turns out the way I want it. But most of all, I learned this turn of events was not a tragedy - it was just life. And it was far better to embrace the adventure of it all.

When you're a single parent, you have to understand and accept what is within your control, what is beyond your control, and find a way to muddle through anyway. One of my dilemmas was needing to make a home where I could be available for my kids, but also bring in income to pay rent and buy groceries. I tried many things -- home businesses, sewing, landscaping. I ran the community toddler gym so my kids could come with me.

It was of paramount importance that my kids were with me while I did this. All the books about helping children through divorce seem to agree that twelve years old is the hardest age for a child to deal with the breakup. My daughter was twelve, and my boys were not far behind. Other women getting divorced had jobs and a system in place so they could keep working, but that wasn't going to work for us, because I'd always been a stay-at-home mom.

I wanted to be a stay-home entrepreneur too, but it takes time to build a home business. Leaving my kids for eight hours a day wasn't an option, not only because of the breakup, but because I couldn't make enough money to pay for daycare for three kids.

Moreover, I had a child who didn't do well with babysitting situations. When I went to the welfare office and asked for help, they told me I would have to attend job seminars and start working. The problem was I had a skill set, but under the circumstances, I couldn't use them in my community.

Imagine living in a small - I mean tiny - town, and everyone knows your husband has "come out" in a big way. Even going to the store became a challenge. People would look at me with their sad eyes. They didn't know what to say or do. Some would blurt out things like, "I always knew he was gay." (Translation: "How could you have been so stupid?")

"Even going to the store became a challenge."

Needless to say, I needed some time and space to heal, and working from home seemed to be the best choice. Some people translated my not wanting to get a job as being lazy. I believed something would work out. I was a life coach when it was a brand new field, and I knew building a business was a process. So I did what I could. I gardened when the kids were in school, and I found a job preparing affidavits for a radio station.

Then the day came when I had to tell my landlady I could no longer afford rent. I would have to move. That's when I humbly said yes to the camper, and a friend found me a job at a real camp nearby. The people in charge accepted me with open arms. They gave me a slot for the trailer and let me work in the kitchen. Problem solved! The kids were with me and had an entire camp for their backyard, and mom was a hop, skip, and a jump away in the kitchen.

My life coach, Patrick Snow, says all great people have times in their lives that look like failure, but it is just a "time" part of the process. Living at camp was a mixed blessing because, though in retrospect it was good in every way, in my mind, I couldn't get past the fact that at this time of my life I was living in a camper with three kids, and it felt like failure.

So I had to reframe it: "I'm on the staff of Lakewood Bible Camp, and my kids are having the summer of their lives!" Learning the fine art of reframing isn't just a word game – it's a valuable life skill.

Reframing requires seeing what is truly there. That old curmudgeon, Henry Ford, said, "Whether you believe you can or can't, you are right." To fully enjoy the adventure of life, we need to approach every day with a sense of awe and wonder. When I realized that what at first felt like failure had become a vacation with a purpose, it was like the first sight of the Grand Canyon. It was so breathtaking that I had to pinch myself to make sure this was reality and not some incredible dream sequence.

Faith is closely connected with hope. I hoped my kids would be full, safe, and happy. I thought that meant a spacious house with a picket fence and a fat bank account, so I didn't see it coming—my hopes were realized on an island campground. When these blessings happen, they're little reminders—tastes of heaven—that help us to trust the next time things seem out of control. See, control kills wonder and discourages faith, trust, and belief.

If we believe something will happen, we can "wonder" and enjoy the journey. Wondering about possibilities opens us to the opportunities that can come our way. Not always, but usually, they are different from how we originally envisioned them. Thank goodness!

I was angling for a job at the high school; it was an attendance position, which seemed perfect. I hoped beyond hope that I would get that job -- I needed that job! That job would solve my problems! But I wasn't even considered for the position. They already had an eye on someone from within the ranks. It was devastating. Kind of funny, what I hoped for didn't work out, so I became hopeless. When the ball didn't bounce my way, I didn't want to play.

What I didn't know was that there was a job for me. Not only was it was better paying, it was more stable, and I was able to do it for four years. Get this: my office was in the high school!

Thank goodness I didn't get what I *thought* I wanted instead of what I *really* wanted. I still struggle with control, but when I wonder, rather than demand something, I have peace, rather than that intense desperation of, "oh, this HAS to work out."

After that job, I was offered an overnight full-time position where I previously worked part-time. It was very difficult to work those hours. I wanted the job, but had my kids been younger I wouldn't have accepted it. The boys werein high school, though, and their sister, who was in a cosmetology program, wanted to move home.

The timing seemed perfect, but we all know no matter how "good" kids are, they can't be home alone all night, every night, because other teens find out. Having their older sister home at night took care of that issue.

Working all night had its own frustrations. I felt like a zombie most of the time, but was able to be awake and available in the evenings before I had to leave. Time and circumstances all play a part when it comes to working.

You know what your family needs. And you know what you can handle, and what they can't handle. Trust what you know, wonder about what could happen, and stand by what you believe in. If you end up in a situation that seems hopeless and dead end, change plans.

Start your plan by believing something better will happen and by wondering about what could be next. Ask yourself what it is you really want, and be open to what it will take to get there. Hire a coach, or get some complimentary coaching calls. I know there are always circumstances that make things harder to make changes. You may have a child with a disability or chronic illness,and you absolutely cannot give up insurance. But we have to have something to dream about, something to look forward to, and to hope for. (The good kind of hope.) We have so many pressures and demands, but we cannot lose sight of what is good and beautiful. Find what you love and fill your cup - then you have something to offer your family.

Life truly is an adventure. Adventure isn't just for those with a dull life looking for a little fun. Adventure is life, and it happens to all of us. We are the character in our story, and we choose how we will participate: Fully? Or dragging our feet? I wonder what sort of tale you've landed in?

Just Wondering:

Back in chapter one you answered the question, "What are your struggles?" Look at them and write how each one might be turned into or looked at as an adventure.

Is there something you want, but it is getting blocked by "shoulds"? "Shoulding" is very dangerous. What "shoulds" do you have rattling around in your head? For single parents, it might be mom or dad guilt. "I should______."

When you really think about the "shoulds" you've written above, are they really true? Example: I should be able to do it all. Really? I give you permission to address these "shoulds" - each one - and speak the truth. "No I SHOULD NOT be able to do it all!" No one can.

What do you know is true for you? Example: No one can do it all- change it to: "This is what I do well." Make a list of what you do well, addressing the "shoulds" and knock them out of the ballpark.

I tend to react out of fear. It was always on the front burner. What fears are you reacting out of? As single parents we have to let go of some things. Others might "should" on us to do more. What can you let go of in spite of what others think?

Although the feeling is so intense, remind yourself of what is true right now, today. Example: "I won't make it financially." Change that to: "Today I am okay." Contiue down the list writing the truth for each fear or should.

4

Asking for help

"Logic is death to that part of you
that is the miracle maker."
- Stuart Wilde

No single parent can navigate the adventure without becoming savvy in the art of asking for, giving, and receiving help. The adventure has begun, and you are choosing to embrace it and wonder about it. Where will it take you and what you will learn? The adventure, and lesson, continues by learning to ask for help. It is excruciatingly difficult at times, but think of it as a sales opportunity.

Learning to ask is teaching you how to present a situation and get what you need. Patricia Fripp, a well-known public speaker and sales guru, teaches that if you don't ask, you don't have the opportunity to encounter what's next. When I wanted so badly to go to her seminar, I couldn't afford it. It didn't occur to me to ask if there was some way I could attend even though I didn't have the money. I was limited by the price, blinded to possibilities.

One of the hardest things to do is *ASK FOR HELP. The second hardest is receiving the help you really need. As my sister would say, "Ask, rather than hint or manipulate, because people can't read your mind."* Asking has so many negatives that go along with it. It "feels" needy, pathetic, like I can't do it all myself. Many sales seminars spend hours teaching us to *ask to get.* You have to ask to even get a no. You never know if something is available if you don't ask. There is a blessing to asking. Something comes up, I need a ride somewhere, and I don't go because I don't think to ask for a ride. My independence gets in the way. I am weary of asking, and yet in the asking I have received great blessings including scholarships, connections, and lifelines.

People aren't always great at helping, not because they're unwilling, but because it can be awkward. Do you just walk up to someone and say, "I'm going to help you?" By asking, we guide people and help them understand how to help us. Sometimes we act like we know what they're able to do, or not do, and what they will inevitably say. But there's really no way to know for sure until you ask. SO, ASK.

Say What You Need

Ask, believing the person *will take care of themselves* and say no if they cannot help. Ask, believing they will take care of themselves and not take on something too big and say yes when they really mean no. If you're the one being asked for help, be honest and say no if you can't meet the need. Trust the one asking is adult enough to find another way, if it's not a possibility for you. There's nothing worse for a relationship than saying yes when you want to say no. It's a one-way street to resentment and anxiety.

We can all handle a "no." *It's okay to say, "No." It's ok to hear, "No."* "No" will not cause anyone to break. We will make our way to a "yes." Just be honest, whether you're asking for or giving help. For the single parent, ask with an attitude that if the person you are addressing can't help, there will be some other resource or idea available. Ask while leaving them room to say, "I can't do that."

Allow them to tell you what they can do. Be gracious, not desperate. It can be hard, especially because we may indeed feel desperate. But that's where faith kicks in. I will be okay; I will find a way. Determination is different from desperation. Trust yourself to figure it out.

"Determination is different from desperation."

When I asked for help and someone said they couldn't, I was usually good with that. Disappointed that my agenda had to be altered, yes, but okay because I am the queen of resourcefulness. What I hated was when I asked for help and the person who couldn't help, would take it upon themselves to slough me off on others. Like, "Oh, I'm sure 'so and so' would help out."

I asked my neighbor, Cheri, for a ride because my car broke down. She said, "Sorry, I won't be around today." I can handle that. But so often, people feel bad for saying no and try to "fix" us. Trust us to figure it out. We asked; you said no; we move on. Folks who ask for help are usually in a complex situation and don't need increased complexity introduced by guilt-ridden people who can't say no. Resist the urge to absolve your guilt by trying to solve my problem, trust that I will figure it out.

I so want to please people, that when someone starts trying to "fix" me and solve my problems, I don't want to be rude, for heaven's sake. But the crux is this: When someone wants to fix me, I translate it as "They think I'm a burden." But I have to remember that other people's fixing is about them, just like my awful fixing stuff is about me. Some folks who know me can't handle the fact that I am struggling, or that anyone is struggling in this uncanny world, and so they have to fix me in order to make themselves feel better. And I know this first hand from my own mistakes. I believe they fear *if something like that can happen to her, it can happen to me*. Maybe, they think, if I deny the possibility it could happen to me, somehow it won't happen. I have learned after many years of feeling bad, mad, and sad at people's attempt to fix me that it is really about them, not me.

Don't get me wrong, I love these people who are the genuine helpers who love you and want you to be okay. They want your life to be easier. There are the meddlers who don't think you have a brain in your head to figure anything out. Then there are the obligated, who feel some sort of responsibility for you so they help you, while mumbling and grumbling the whole time.

"Because really, who would want a washed up 40-year-old with three kids, a gay ex and a big dog?"

A friend of mine *forced* her husband to help me. I needed wood, and she told him in no uncertain terms he *was* to help me. He let me know that he'd rather be watching the game. He also felt it was his responsibility to let me know I should not get my hopes up about ever meeting a man. Because really, who would want a washed up 40-year-old with three kids, a gay ex and a big dog? That made my day- NOT!

Now, let's talk about the guilt that comes with saying, instead of hearing, "No." It can be even harder to handle, especially when guilt shows up with her friend, fixing.

For example, a single mom I know, a very good friend who works full time, was struggling to pay rent. I wanted to help, but I didn't have the money. It started haunting me. I thought about posting something about it on Facebook to see if someone might donate to her cause. Then I had to think about what it would be like if someone took on my case in that way.

When I mentioned it to a co-worker, before I could even get to the part about me wanting to "rescue" and post the need on FB, the coworker was printing out job possibilities. I'm ashamed to say this, but I forwarded them to my friend.

The problem wasn't that she needed a job. She had one. The issue was that her rent was due and she didn't have it. Based on the Golden Rule, I knew better and had to apologize for my insensitivity.

The thing is, I wanted to help, but this was her story. Instead of wondering what would happen and believing in her, I got caught up in the "Oh no, what is she going to do?" trap. She is the most amazing, resourceful person I know, but I didn't trust her. I let the situation absorb me and wanted to "fix" it. That was so disrespectful.

If I had the resources and chose to help her out that would be different. But I was feeling helpless, and "took" on her issue, even though it wasn't my story. Somehow, some way, her rent and utilities got paid. She figured it out. If it didn't work out that way, then I could be there to help by being supportive, not fixing. It's her adventure, and she's living it beautifully.

Here Is Your Permission Slip

I don't have to let people "should" on me!

I am free to say "No, thanks. I'll pass."

I have a big red circle with the word "FIXING" in the middle and a red line through it!

Put your needs out there anyway, hard as it may be. When I needed a car, I asked around. Yes, I was offered clunkers, because beggars can't be choosers. I was also offered nice vehicles. When I needed a new couch, which seemed to be often, I was offered all kinds of couches. Some were in better shape than others, and I learned to be grateful and still say "No, thank you," when I needed to.

Bartering is a great way to ask for help while offering help. I had great success in bartering; I would trade sewing and gardening for things I needed. Sometimes I would make an actual trade, but what I discovered is if I helped others, then others helped me. If I had a friend who need alterations or help in the garden and I could help them, there always seemed to be someone to help me when I needed it. It's the way the world works. Give and receive. I could get technical and say I have to charge for all my services. When it's a business, that's a good idea, but there is always room for giving.

What do you have that you can trade or barter?

I was a single mom who was barely making it when someone brought me two huge jars of peanut butter from Costco. My neighbor was also a struggling single parent, so I gave her family one of the jars. Guess what? We may have run out of a lot of things, but we never ran out of peanut butter or ramen noodles.

Some people give everything away because they don't think they deserve nice things. This is not what I'm talking about. It isn't being a martyr; it's sharing what we have--doing life together.

It's like the old story about stone soup. I had a friend lovingly challenge me to consider not tithing because I had so little income. I don't believe in telling others what I give or how I give, but I'll tell anyone who asks how important it is to be part of a giving community. There's a verse in the Bible that says to cast our bread on the water and it will come back to us. Someone may say, "Who wants soggy bread?" but the verse is about how you have to give to receive. This is how the real world works. Give-receive, receive-give, ebb and flow: there is a season for all of this. Jesus said to "Use your money to make friends that when the money fails, you will have friends who can care for you."

"Give-receive, receive-give, ebb and flow..."

The recent huge disasters of this century, like the Twin Towers in New York, Hurricane Katrina, and the earthquake in Haiti all caused great devastation, but they also produced an outpouring of human generosity. Something tugs at our hearts, so we give to help someone else, but their receiving is giving something that breathes life into us as well. So let others help! It gives them the opportunity to serve and feel their blessing matters. In receiving, others are blessed.

We've always heard "It is more blessed to give than receive," and in context, I believe that is true. However, learning to receive can be very difficult. Being a gracious receiver takes some practice. I have become a better giver because of learning to receive.

My friend, Marlee, told me a story about meeting a woman who was a single mom who had learned how to receive, and was teaching others the art. Marlee invited her to do a workshop at her house with her friends. Roxy, the single mom, asked who in the group were "givers." Everyone raised their hand. Then she asked how many considered themselves "receivers." One lady raised her hand and said something along the lines of, "Yes, I can receive. I have learned to accept what is given."

So Roxy asked one of the "givers" and the "receiver" to come up front; she gave them each an empty cup. Then she came by with her own cup full of water and asked the giver. "Can I give you some water?" She said, "Oh no, I'm fine." Then she went to the receiver and asked, "Can I give you some water?" She said, "Sure!"

Roxy left and then came back and said, "This is now a different scenario. I am coming from the desert and I am parched." She walked up to the giver and said, "Do you have some water? I am so thirsty and I need a drink." The woman looked at her cup and could only say, "No, I don't have any water." Then Roxy went to the receiver and asked, "Do you have some water? I'm so thirsty." You already know her answer: A resounding "Sure!" As she poured her cup into Roxy's.

"I allow others to bless me because that is how they are blessing God."

When people offer good things, or something out of their barely making it lives, accept. This is different than accepting something from someone who thinks we should just take the stinky couch – we're talking about something they would want for themselves. Accept good things, saying "Yes!" rather than "Oh no, I can't let you do that." I allow others to bless me because that is how they are blessing God. When we are unwilling to receive, we rob others of an opportunity. I rob myself of a future opportunity to give when, in my pride, I turn down generosity.

I Have Pasta. What Do You Have?

Feel like you are in a phase of life where you want to give, but have to receive? Keep in mind that *this too shall pass*. This is just a period of time. It's not forever.

Remember when you had that first baby? Everyone says enjoy this time in your life; it goes fast. Then you have two babies, both in diapers, and it doesn't occur to you that someday you won't have to choose between buying coffee or diapers, because they will outgrow diapers.

Parenting is all-consuming and NOW is very present, especially when struggling to pay rent, put food on the table, and spend time with the kids. This, too, shall pass. Eventually, they grow up and we become empty nesters. There is a season and a reason for every cycle of life.

You really can give even, when it feels like all you can do is receive. Ask and know you can give back, no matter what or when. You always have something to offer, even though it may feel like less than nothing to you.

I remember someone needing pants hemmed. It was so easy for me and took five minutes. When she had her born-again trousers, she raved about my talent, and swore undying gratitude! Wow! Who knew a simple thing I could do in my sleep could help someone else?

What can you offer? A ride, a simple skill, an entree? What seems so simple anyone could do it, when in actuality it is a gift you can give? What comes to you so easily that you assume others can do it too? How about singing lessons for a child of a single parent, piano lessons, gardening, woodcarving, or baking lessons? What do you do that is so mindless or easy that you tend to devalue it?

Part of the point of all this giving and receiving is that we need each other. My friend Jennifer is the single mom of two amazing young women. We met on the overnight shift at the radio station where we worked. I so admired and loved her because of her commitment to her girls. She was a dedicated mom, who was completely on her own. She wanted to be super mom, do it all, have it all, and be it all.

She finally broke down when she became critically ill. When she was hospitalized she *had* to ask for help. It was difficult, but she did it for her kids. I remember her plan because she named it "STONEHENGE" in honor of her kidney stones!

She listed all her friends and their role in the upcoming hospitalization, down to who would call her mom and ex mother-in-law after surgery. I finally got to meet some of her special friends, and it was a blessing for me to help someone. I was so grateful to be part of the Stonehenge retreat.

I remember Jennifer telling me, after the fact, that landing in the hospital was when she was able to let go and accept love from others. She calls it "saying yes to all good things." We're in this together, and this is how we survive and thrive.

Thank you, Jenn, for letting us be a part of "Stonehenge!"

You have enough.

You are enough.

And you do enough.

Sometimes receiving is in the form of a fresh perspective just when you need it. I remember one day when I was really struggling - finances were tight and I thought we weren't going to make it. My friend, Precious, came over and could see my despair. She walked me to the cupboards and asked if we had enough food for today. We took an "enough tour" of my home to show me *there was enough for today*.

Years later, when I didn't even have a home to live in, I could break it down and honestly say, "I have enough for today." Worrying about tomorrow robs you of today.

Now, all of that is "yesterday" and we made it—somehow we made it. I thought, "*You will make it.* **Y**ou are amazing and resourceful, remarkable, resilient, and you will make it. You are doing it, maybe not how you thought you would. But look at you, you have enough; you are enough; and you do enough." There is something I can give, because I received.

Maybe you struggle with depression like me; maybe you have a disorder that makes life harder. Between my children and me, we have many disorders, but we got through it! We didn't make it in a way that I thought it would go, but we did, and you will, too.

There is still something you can give. My daughter talks to youth about growing up in a divorced family with a gay dad. She shares her experience of being homeless and living in a camper. She doesn't describe exactly the same adventure her brothers remember. It is her own story and now she can bring hope to children of divorce.

One of my sons had a near death experience because of some bad choices, and I almost lost him on Mothers' Day. During his remaining years at high school, he talked with middle school kids about making bad choices and the price you pay. But most of all he tells them the long difficult journey of winning back the respect of adults in his life: teachers, coaches, friends, parents, neighbors, and even relatives.

I would never have chosen this life for my family. But no matter what, we were a family and we still are. We made the best of a difficult situation–even thriving, not just surviving. And you can, too. You will.

When you don't give up on the adventure that leads to your dream, it means in part that you have learned how to ask, give, and receive. Even when you don't have material resources, you always have the wisdom gained from experiencing life in all its many facets. What you have to offer others in work, word, or task is priceless. Reach out. Offer what you have, and I bet you will be surprised.

I can't tell you how many people I have taught to sew. Would I want to do it for a living? No, but for survival? Yes. I've altered all kinds of clothes: Prom and wedding dresses, handbags, shirts, and socks. I discovered a resource in sewing. I enjoy it, and I used it as a survival tool. What do you have? What can you offer the world? There is the "for now" and the bigger picture. This week I actually saw sunshine in Seattle (Imagine that!) and posted a message on Facebook: "I planted flowers and soaked up some sun." Say what you will about Facebook, I was giving something of myself in that comment. The comments I received in response became cherished memories. People remembered my policy with my garden and how I gave blooms and produce away to everyone and anyone. I had no money to offer, but I took flowers from my garden to every occasion imaginable. I used what I had, and it seemed so insignificant at the time.

Don't "dis" what you have, even if it is just a jar of peanut butter, a flower, or a needle and thread. Give what you have. One time my kids got together and pooled their pennies, offering to help pay for something. It was only pennies: small change! It was all the money they had, but more than that, it represented their hearts. They wanted to contribute. I gave of what I had and always wished it was more, bigger, greater. But the act of giving out of my poverty kept me in the game. It kept me feeling like I could contribute, and I would be okay as long as I could be helping in some way, somehow. I always underestimated my gift; it never felt like enough. But I was wrong. It was everything.

"Don't "dis" what you have, even if it is just a jar of peanut butter, a flower, or a needle and thread."

Who you are and what you have to offer this world, your community, your neighborhood, your family is unique. It doesn't go away. It's still there just waiting to be cultivated. My family came first, and my dream waited while I stayed true to my values. You know what? "Life happening" (daily life) became part of my "what's next."

The Journey Matters

The whole time when I felt like I was treading water, trying not to drown, watching my hopes and dreams sail off without me, they were just up river a little. Now they're accepting me back with open arms and asking to hear the stories of a broken heart. Raising three amazing children on a shoestring seemed like a detour on the way to my dreams, but guess what? *The journey matters.* Even now, this new phase is only another leg of the journey. You don't give up your dream when life seems to get in the way. Let it change, shape, and mold around you, because your dream is you.

Ask, share, barter, and don't give in to "shoulds" - yours or anyone else's. Be involved in life. Make it happen. Don't wait for good things; they're happening all around you. Find a way. Don't get caught up in "I can't because." If you're making your life happen, you begin to remember your dream, because you're being active in your life. I may think I don't have enough money, time, or me to go around. That is when I realize I have a community that wants to bless me if I am willing to give them a chance.

"That is when I realize I have a community that wants to bless me if I am willing to give them a chance."

I also realize how good I feel when I can give back, or help someone else without sacrificing my family. It made me realize I am not alone. I didn't have to hide out because of the shame of having little to offer; I had to choose to be a part of a community, rather than live in a vacuum. Find your community, learn to receive, and let others be blessed by your graciousness.

Just Wondering:

Have you ever had a situation where you offered something from your heart, and the person couldn't receive?

How did that make you feel?

What would you have liked to happen?

How are you at receiving?

When have you said no, when you could have said yes?

What kept you from saying yes?

Will you look for opportunities to say yes?

Have you lost sight of your dream?

Too late?

Too hard?

Who me? If not you, then who?

Do you remember it? What was it?

What was it you wanted to be when you grew up, before life happened?

What was the big plan, before life got in the way?

I'm asking you to remember and believe it is waiting.

Write a day in the life of your dream--morning to evening.

5
The Validation Game

"I often sailed away to naps to repair from my perfectionism, procrastination or the voices of the inner critic shouting... 'you'll never make it.'"

- SARK (Susan Ariel Rainbow Kennedy)

Even in embracing community and finding resources, there will be times when you feel like you don't bring enough to the table. It's when you feel like the story you landed in is someone else's, because the demands on your resources are way beyond what you have to give. Sometimes I felt like a fraud because I continued functioning as Mom, but it seemed like someone else out there could provide all the things I couldn't.... So the question becomes, "How do you not give in to the lie—yes lie--of not being enough, having enough, or doing enough?"

"How do you not give in to the lie—yes lie--of not being enough, having enough, or doing enough?"

I was immediately put in the position of feeling inadequate the instant I became a single mom. The load was so much lighter when there were two of us to shoulder it. I want to do more for my children. I want to have more influence in their lives. I didn't feel I was enough to meet all their needs. But I have come to realize I am enough, I do enough, and we have enough. It is not about having it all and doing it all, but about doing what I can and being grateful for what I can provide. I spent many hours feeling sad for what I couldn't give my kids. Yet they were always grateful for what they did get.

You are enough.

You have enough.

You do enough.

I wanted to take them camping, on vacations, and to other countries. I wanted to provide snowboarding opportunities for my sons and horse opportunities for my daughter. wished they could have had more than I could offer.

I did attempt to take the boys fishing; but I wasn't very good at it. I wished there was someone who would take them out and really teach them how to angle. Little did I realize they would have an opportunity I would never have thought of.

It happened like this: When the kids were little, we lived on a farm with a pond. One day, the five-year-old neighbor boy came over and saw my sons lying by the side of the pond with sticks and rope "fishing." Needless to say, their technique was lacking. So the neighbor boy, Austin, ran home and got a fish he had caught the week before. It was frozen, but he took it out of the freezer, brought it back to the pond, and tied it to the rope of my older son, without him knowing it! Then he tugged on the line like a fish would, and my son

Davis reeled in a very stiff catch! Davis could hardly wait to tell me about the *frozen* fish he caught in the lake.

Through the years the boys' longings included more than fish. First it was ATVs, then motorcycles, and finally cars. Children of wealthier parents had these sorts of things, but I couldn't afford even a toy version of their dream rides. I felt badly about not being the kind of parent who could write a check for a car, but my sons never complained. They come from resourceful stock, remember, so they worked and saved until they got what they wanted. It was better that way in the end.

For example, my son, Davis, needed six hundred dollars to pay off his school before they would let him graduate. I couldn't give it to him. Mr. Resourceful, he found grants and scholarships and worked for the rest.

He graduated. I'm so proud, but I spent a lot of time playing the "should" game: "I should help him; what kind of mother can't help her son?" The crazy thing is he doesn't feel that way at all! He's *proud* that he was able to save up and pay it off and graduate. It means more to him that he did it. I would have paid if I could have, but it wasn't a possibility for me, and yet he found a way to make it happen.

When my daughter was getting married, I couldn't afford a wedding. I suffered so much guilt. But Jenna's resourceful, too, and she figured it all out and had the best wedding I've ever been to. She and her husband found a way to make it happen with the help of church and community. She went on to school and got scholarships and grants and made it happen. She was all right with my limitations, and told me not to worry.

My youngest son just graduated. He suffered the death of a friend while he was still in high school. I wanted to be there for him, but he didn't need me. He is handling it. I spend a lot of time feeling guilty when the truth is Danen is an amazing young man who is ready to take on the world. He's funny and compassionate and independent.

"What are you struggling with?"

I raised these kids to be resourceful; but despite my worry that I wasn't enough, they took what they learned and found ways to do what they needed to do. I wasn't able to provide much in the way of resources but I did support them and believed in them. I wanted to do so much more, but it turned out to be enough. Stop worrying about what you can't provide, and focus on what you CAN provide.

What are you struggling with? Where do you feel a lack? Is it possible you *are* enough? Even if they aren't getting what you think they need? Is loving, supporting, and believing in your kids enough?

Asking for help and connecting it to "being enough" is a gift you give yourself. What makes us "enough" is the support we have--the friends and love in our lives, giving and receiving. It takes both.

The Washington State Readiness to Learn program (RTL) counts those living in bedrooms with family as homeless. If that definition is correct, I know homelessness. That shocked me because when I think of the homeless, I think of people on the streets of Seattle. They live in doorways, under bridges, and freeway overpasses. We even have a place called the jungle where the homeless in Seattle live. We don't think of families *in transition* as homeless, but they are, in fact, homeless. Having to live with others because we have nowhere else to go makes us homeless.

I became homeless when I could no longer pay rent because of my choice to be with my kids and work from home. That's when we lived in a camper for six months. During this time of transition, I discovered there were funds available. I was able to get gas vouchers and my kids qualified for free lunch, school supplies, and various other services--such as Readiness to Learn, a particularly helpful program, focused on keeping homeless kids from falling through the cracks. These services relied on grants, but it became tougher and tougher to get the grants as the state's economy plummeted. But somehow we made it.

We became homeless again a few years later. One summer my daughter stayed with her dad, my boys stayed with my sister, and I stayed nearby in my own small space. I worked as a gardener, and my goal was to get us all settled in time for school to start. Family was great during that time. I knew I always had a place with my brother and his wife or my sister and her husband. They would take me in in a heartbeat. My kids wanted to stay near their dad, and I wanted to maintain the fleeting opportunity to provide a home for as long as possible. I also wanted to respect their wishes by letting them have both parents close at hand.

That homeless season only lasted a few months until I got a job and our farm rental house back. Now the kids were older and I only worked while they were at school. I learned a lot about homelessness through the resource center. The most remarkable thing I felt was that they treated me, a homeless mother, with dignity. They had helped me during my time of need, and later I was able to help as a volunteer at the center. It was incredible. In fact, it was because of that positive experience that I went back to school and got a degree in social services.

A blessing of trials is learning the suffering side of the story and becoming available to others in a completely different way. When women came into the center to seek help, I was able to tell them from experience that it was going to be okay. I was enough to make it, and so were they.

Now, I'm the Queen of Resources. You can ask me *anything* about available resources. Go ahead! If I don't know the answer, I'll find it! People want to help. There are organizations everywhere for almost anything; energy assistance organizations, food banks, food stamps, and housing assistance groups like HUD, (which had a five-year waiting list for people who needed housing, and I made the top of the list—twice!)

You will need perseverance, though. Many times I went to different agencies with kids in tow, telling my story over and over, and filling out mounds of paperwork and just to be told to wait. Finally, I found the local Family Resource Center. It became my lifeblood.

Gail was an innovative director who would ask us, the needy, what worked and what didn't. She was interested in us, not just in fulfilling her job description. She thought we each had something to offer. It was also Gail who encouraged me to apply for a job that I thought was way out of my league when I didn't have a degree. Because of Gail's belief in me combined with perseverance, I was able to get the job the second time around.

Speaking of perseverance, Gail met with directors of all the charities in the community that included us, the "access-ors" of services. She wanted us to have a say in how resources were allotted and what services were offered. One accomplishment was the establishment of a "traveling application." Now a family only has to fill out one application for all the charities. This let us bypass the mountains of redundant paperwork, without having to repeat our sad songs over and over again.

That helped, but there was still much to be done to restore homeless people to their God-given dignity. At one of these community meetings, Gail surprised me with a special opportunity to be of help. Just as the meeting was about to adjourn, Gail looked at me and said, "It's almost time to go, but we haven't heard from Laurie yet." So I stood up and asked how many of them worked as volunteers in an organization offering services. Everyone raised her hand. There was such a sense of pride and good cheer.

Then I asked them to leave their hand up if they have ever accessed any of these services for themselves. Just one hand remained up. I said, "You all love to help. It is evident and wonderful. It may be hard for you to understand us, but what looks like ungratefulness is shame. We would much rather be in your shoes. We don't want to be paraded through the office or service center so everyone can see we're needy."

I offered the illustration of our food bank. It was set up in such a way that food recipients had to pass through the thrift store at the front of the building in full view of all their bargain-hunting friends, who could then watch them enter, collect a cardboard box of donated items, and carry it back through the retail area and out. People were grateful for the food, but also embarrassed and ashamed about needing help.

That has now changed, and I like to think my little talk had a small part in the new arrangement. Not only has the food bank moved to a remote property, there are other wonderful changes – such as the fact that people actually get to shop, like in a regular market, and with increased options, folks have a choice about what their family will eat.

A few years later at another meeting, a lady came up to me and thanked me. She told me she was at that meeting when I spoke, and it had never before occurred to her how it must feel to be in our shoes. Not only did I have the opportunity to receive resources, but it was also an unexpected opportunity to offer something that would make the system and people's lives better.

I talk a lot about giving and sharing resources. It's important to be in community and to be able to give back when possible. A single mom actually gave me the words to find my place with giving: I believe in giving even when it seems like I have nothing to give. I believe in sharing, or trading, with others.

Crystal was a friend and also a single parent dealing with cancer - and she was brilliant at recruiting people to help her through this difficult time. It was quite a process even before surgery. I was so proud to be on her list of helpers; it felt good to be walking with her through such a scary time. We were talking about giving and helping out others, and she told me that she can get overwhelmed with giving.

She's grateful for all the help, but if she's not careful, she almost sabotages her family by helping others too much. She pointed out that many people have a guideline about giving ten percent of their financial resources, and she incorporates that into her time-giving, as well. Sometimes you feel guilty or obligated to help because you've been helped, but it's easy to go overboard, and then the family suffers.

Wise words from such a young lady. In retrospect, I know there were times I was so busy trying to help everyone else that I didn't have very good boundaries about when to call it a day. Crystal found that delicate balance between giving and receiving that keeps her family as top priority.

"Crystal found that delicate balance between giving and receiving that keeps her family as top priority."

Remember I said we lived on a farm? Well, it was a racehorse farm and the resident horses lived there between racing seasons. When I first moved there, I did almost everything for the horses. Besides feeding them and mucking out the barn, I met with the veterinarians, the farrier, and the horse haulers. I was paid for my time. But when I took a full-time job, I could no longer keep those random appointments, and so I had to hand off those duties.

Later, when money was tight, friends would suggest I ask the landlord if there were things I could do in trade, but I only had so much time. I worked full time and had three kids at home who each had their activities. There had to be limits to how much I could do.

There were also times that people would offer me, say, firewood, or perhaps a small job that I had to turn down because I absolutely couldn't work it into my schedule. I felt badly because I knew some people thought, "Wow, we hear she has needs and we offered her an opportunity to make money and she turned us down!" It was difficult to say no, and I worried people would think I wasn't trying hard enough. I was fighting to keep my family together and had to consider my children's needs, which included having mom present and available at the right time, plus working to keep food on the table.

Both those times were important to my mission, and sometimes, small jobs subtracted from the operation, even while they added to the coffers. Another single mom I knew was working two jobs already, but was offered an additional job for ten dollars an hour. She politely declined. The person who told her about the job was appalled, but my friend said, "It is just not worth it. I am already exhausted and have nothing left for my kids, or my church. I cannot take on another job." I was so proud of her!

By being true to who she was called to be, she was keeping the door open to better possibilities. Sometimes the piecework leads to less time for the real goal -- family - and takes away from the little we already have.

"Logic is death to that part of you that is the miracle maker." - *Stuart Wilde*

We want to be logical and don't want to be hopeless dreamers. But there is a time when all the logic in the world doesn't make it work or make good things happen. Sometimes we have to fall back on our faith and believe and wonder what will happen. We can only do so much; we can only be so much, and our kids need us.

Sometimes we have to use our creative juices to make the most of what we have. Maybe we will lose our homes or our rentals. But is that the worst thing that could happen? It may feel like it, but maybe not having enough will move us to a place that is ultimately a "better" or different place that represents another leg of the adventure.

Over extending ourselves to keep what we have may not be the answer. I remember watching a documentary about housing projects. The parents were bussed out to work so they had about a two hour commute each way, and then they worked eight hours, but really nine when you included the lunch hour. Twelve hours of their day was taken in working and traveling.

Something happened with the children left at home. They got in trouble, many were put in juvenile halls, and the parent was shamed for not being there. I remember thinking, "What other option did she have? It was such a vicious cycle with no way to get out." I haven't been in that situation, so I'm not saying that I could have done anything differently. Logically, there was no other option; the parent had to work to live in the building.

I had to believe with all my heart that something would work out. Somehow, some way, even though it didn't make any sense, something had to work out. I had to leave the door open for some possibilities by believing I would make it. Just taking any and every job wasn't the solution, despite the inevitable judgment and misunderstanding that would come.

One of the more difficult things was that people who had never been in my situation regularly said they didn't understand me. They didn't know what it was like to tell your kids you're having ramen for dinner again. They didn't know what it was like to not buy your kids' school pictures. They had no idea what it was like to have to go to everything alone, all the time.

They couldn't understand why I couldn't do a ladies night out. I couldn't afford babysitting, and I certainly couldn't afford dinner out. It was hard to say I was too busy when people would ask me out to lunch and I couldn't afford it.

I did sack lunches often with my friend Wendy or we would split something. When you don't have the time, money, or babysitting, then you don't go and do anything. You stay home. And sometimes it was really hard watching other people have a life and do fun things, like taking the kids to the zoo or the science center. It all costs money.

I did, however, come up with a list of free things to do and we did them a lot. We went to flower nurseries with walking trails and took snacks for the kids. We swam at the beach, not the pool, and took sack lunches. Thank goodness we didn't have the ice cream truck driving by—that may have been too many no's for me to handle!

"We went to flower nurseries with walking trails and took snacks for the kids."

I hated being misunderstood, but if I actually said I couldn't afford it, they would often offer to pay. This was wonderful of them, but really hard for me. How do you order? What do you order, the cheapest thing on the menu? I know it may sound like ingratitude, but if you've been in that position, you know how embarrassing it is.

After this, my worst fears were often realized when people just stopped inviting me. Nevertheless, I was in life, and my kids and I had each other; and despite all we couldn't do, it was a good life. I now know that I was enough. Many famous people were raised by single moms, often with very humble beginnings.

When I mention I'm a single parent, people often tell me they were raised by a single mom or dad. They seem to be grateful for all their parent did for them. They also seem to have great respect for that parent. There are exceptions, of course. Certainly some were abandoned, neglected, abused, or left alone to fend for themselves.

I've heard more stories than I like to admit about kids raised by single parents who were way more interested in dating than nurturing the kids. It is easy for a single parent to end up in a bad relationship. What does it cost the kids? Are they being abused? Is it really worth dating and re-marrying at the kids' expense? I'm not judging, just asking.

I made mistakes, but when push came to shove, my kids came first. For awhile, I didn't believe I was enough, and I was looking for someone to fill that gap. I didn't want to raise kids alone – I wanted help! But ultimately, I chose to be a single parent rather than get sucked into another relationship that could be harmful to us; and their childhood went by so fast. I thought a single-parent home wasn't good for the children, but I was wrong. I had to accept that I was enough and could "outsource" what I couldn't give.

"It is easy for a single parent to end up in a bad relationship."

That meant, for example, Big Brother/Big Sister and other ways of meeting their needs. Rather than trying to fill a void by finding a partner, I found friends that fit that description. My kids call my friend, Laurie D., their other mother. She fixed their cars, had talks with them, but most of all, she was always around. She was a neighbor who would often stop by for coffee and a visit. She got the gist of how our family worked and she loved my kids. During those times as a parent when I wanted to share a small triumph, I knew if I called Laurie she would be excited for my kids. If they were having problems, she asked questions, listened, and helped them figure out how to resolve their issues themselves, while being supportive and loving.

Other times I didn't feel so alone because of friends like Cousin Donna. She lived down the road; she was actually my kids' cousin and my friend. Beside my kids, Donna was one of the best things I got out of my marriage.

"The boys met her at the door with their BB guns."

One night we were scared, thinking someone was on the roof, trying to get into our house. I called Donna and she got to the house within minutes. The boys met her at the door with their BB guns. She and I walked around the house and discovered the intruder was apples! Our big old apple tree was dropping apples on the roof. We laughed, and she never condemned me because I got her out of a warm bed.

Another time I came home to discover our beloved dog couldn't move. I called the horse vet to come over because Bear was too big for me to lift into a car. At the time, Bear was 12 or 13 with failing health I had a decision to make, and I knew what it was supposed to be. I was very brave until I went in the house to call Donna and ask her to please come over – and then I could barely speak, I was crying so hard.

My neighbor Wilma came over too, and the three of us gathered around Bear in a "bear hug" and said goodbye to the dear old boy. I can't imagine if I had to do that alone. I've been so blessed with people and programs coming into our lives to fill in some of the gaps.

Not everything gets filled in; sometimes we just have to live with things the way they are, like cars that don't run so well. (God bless AAA!) We had washers and dryers that would break down, and had to wait for someone like our friend Mike, who knew how to fix things, to show up when he had time. Sometimes we had disappointments and disagreements that seem like they would take us down for the final count. But we survived and become better people in the process.

I will never forget telling the school counselor about what our life was like. I was trying to paint a picture for her because one of my kids was really struggling. I told about the divorce, the coming out, my remarriage, and all the pain. She looked at me and said of my daughter, "That poor baby." I was so touched that she could acknowledge what my child had been through, and at the same time, it was amazing that she was talking about my kid.

"As I look back I wonder 'Was I enough?'"

We had talked about everything our family had been through, and I thought my kids were quite well adjusted. We were stronger for the struggles, although I would have never chosen them for my family. As I look back I wonder "Was I enough?" I was, and thankfully I wasn't. Together, we were enough. Together, meaning my kids, myself, our family, our friends, and our community. We made it together.

I heard Carol Kent speak at a convention about her book called, *A New Kind of Normal.* She is a well known Christian speaker and writer. Her life fell apart when her son was convicted of murder and sentenced to life in prison. What I loved and hated about her story was that there was no "happy ending." She said people would tell her they were praying for her son to get out of prison and telling her to just believe, but the fact was, any possibility of a pardon had passed and her son was (is) there to stay.

What a brave woman to get up and talk about a story with no happy ending. No resolution, no miracle. He is her only son, and he's in prison. The point isn't about what he did or didn't do, the point is there are things in life that are unsolvable.

There are situations with bad endings. There are women in abusive situations, and they can't get out. When they try to escape, sometimes they get killed. I know women who stay in abusive situations because they are paralyzed, or they know without a doubt the price to pay for getting out is too much. It may cost them their children, or their lives. There are difficult situations, and people living through them are often very misunderstood.

When I worked at KSPD in Boise, Idaho, I interviewed Joni Erikson Tada. She was paralyzed in a swimming accident when she was a teenager. Using a pen in her mouth, she draws pictures, makes cards, sings, and also speaks all over the country. She has made a huge impact in improving the lives of the handicapped.

Her attitude toward her disability and life in general was AMAZING, and I was blown away by her joy and acceptance of what had happened to her. Two weeks prior to my interview with Joni, I interviewed a couple known for "faith healing." They told me Joni is a friend of theirs, and they always tell her if she had enough faith she could walk. When I met Joni, I asked her what she does with situations like this. She said, "God bless them, I know my life is making a difference; and if God wanted me walking I would be." Such grace! Some situations are not solvable.

Friends of mine have a child who is severely autistic. She's much like a single parent because she's alone so much. Although she has three other children, the one with autism can be totally consuming. There is no "solving" the problem; there is no "making it better." People offer her solutions all the time. I don't know her pain, but I have asked her how she copes, and she says sometimes it is really hard. Her son is never going to grow up, get married, and move away. And as he gets bigger, it's harder for her to help him or keep him from hurting himself. She is loving and gracious, and yet she gets to her wits ends at times.

I know people who have adopted kids with fetal alcohol syndrome. They get well-meaning advice about "getting tough" with these kids. Really? Their friends don't understand. Some even accuse them of making up excuses, and even some "friends" have tried to "rescue" the poor child from the mean parents. This rescue scenario never lasts very long, because typical rescuers have no endurance. The kids look normal, and for the most part, are very functional, but there is something that doesn't connect because they are actually brain-damaged. They literally cannot think the way most people do, and they don't understand consequences.

What these families have experienced is people swooping in to tell them how to parent, and blaming the parents if the child doesn't get certain basic concepts of life. The prognosis for kids with this syndrome is at best inability to hold down a job, and at worst jail, homelessness, addiction, and suicide.

There are some stories that just will not have a happy ending. If you're living it, find a support system. Find something that helps you get free from the guilt that drains and paralyzes you. If you know someone living with an unsolvable situation, try to validate their feelings before offering unsolicited advice. Think outside of your usual mode of operation: Try to understand, and not fix the situation. What that parent needs more than anything is someone who believes their story and believes in them. The last thing they need is to be blamed for things outside their control.

Validation is a "free" and life-giving gift. "I told you so" is death. I don't know why we feel the need to make ourselves feel better at someone else's expense. After having a miscarriage, I learned a lot about validation. The things people would say left me feeling worse about myself, my situation, and my God. A miscarriage is unsolvable. It just is. It is a very difficult cross to bear. With all the wonderful pat answers people deliver, it is a wonder anyone with any kind of situation like that ever shows their face in public again.

"Validation is a "free" and life-giving gift."

Don't tell me it was meant to be. Don't tell me God wanted that baby more than I did. Don't say things that make you feel better; say nothing or validate the pain, like, "This must be hard. I'm so sad this happened to you." And if the person suffering from the injustice tries to offer you solace by saying, "It must not have been the right timing," or something ridiculous like that, intervene and say, "No! This is a terrible thing that has happened."

When we are validated we can let go; if we have to defend ourselves, it actually makes things worse. This is true for kids, too. Validate their feelings and frustrations. Validation is a wonderful tool for you to believe you are enough. You can't fix, but you can validate, and that is the truest gift. You are enough, you have enough, and you do enough. That is what the adventure is all about.

Find ways to let go of your own expectations
of what enough looks like.
It looks like you.
You are enough.

Just Wondering:

How can you find peace with being "enough"?

What expectations can you let go of, to be "okay" with what you do offer?

In what ways are you enough?

List ten:

1

2

3

4

5

6

7

8

9

10

What are ways you have been helped with dignity?

How is your give/receive balance?

Are you giving too much?

Not enough?

Too often?

What do your boundaries around giving look like?

You may need permission to "not give too much" of your time, money, and resources.

What are some of the ways you feel misunderstood?

When have you felt validated?'

What was it like?

I wonder if there is someone you know who is really struggling and could benefit from some validation?

Who?

How might you validate them?

Never underestimate the power of validation.

6
Knowing What You Know

"I feel there are two people inside me - me and my intuition. If I go against her, she'll screw me every time, and if I follow her, we get along quite nicely."
- Kim Basinger

"Intuition will tell the thinking mind where to look next."
-Jonas Salk

Once you begin to accept that you are enough, have enough, and do enough, you will have more energy to put toward what you know. You will have the stamina to trust that in being enough, you have a sense of what you know and what you believe. You will begin to trust what you know.

This is so important as a single woman because you have to trust your instincts and be able to protect yourself and sense when things aren't right. Accepting being enough gives you more energy to put in this direction. Know what you know and trust your instincts.

"*Know what you know*" is one of my favorite sayings. I had to relearn to trust my instincts. I say "relearn" because we are born with instincts but we're taught not to trust them. We're told we are thinking too much, overreacting, or even crazy. I spent a period of time getting in touch with my instincts and began to trust what I knew.

"Know what you know and trust your instincts."

I recommend a book by Gavin de Becker called *The Gift of Fear*. De Becker talks about the mind's ability to "know" things you don't know you know. He tells of stories about women who have been assaulted or raped, and they almost always say in retrospect, "I knew something was wrong."

As a single parent, you have to not only trust your instincts, but nurture your children to trust theirs as well. This means validating them, believing them, and helping them understand what instinct is and how valuable it is.

I used to work with a blind man named Randy. He was amazing. He worked in radio as a sports broadcaster, played rock and roll on the piano, and walked to and from work. Randy had a wonderful sense of humor, and I loved working with him.

One day, he was walking down the hall when I saw him coming toward me, and I just stopped, right in the middle of the hall, and waited quietly for him. Before he got to me, he swerved while I stayed still, and he went around me. After he passed, I called, "Hey, Randy!" My voice startled him a bit. I asked if he knew I was standing in his way. He said, "No." So I asked him why he went around me. He said he wasn't sure, but *somehow he knew* there was a barrier.

The problem with trusting your instincts and avoiding potentially dangerous things is that you never really know that you avoided anything. If you have a feeling not to go somewhere and you don't go, you don't know what would have happened. So you don't know if you were being silly or if there was really a deeper reason you didn't go. Trust your instincts anyway. Trust what you know, even if you don't know why or how you know it.

It bears repeating: Believe in yourself and trust what you know. Our instincts won't keep us from all danger, but there are times where I just feel something on a deeper level.

I work in downtown Seattle and get finished very late. There are times when something inside prompts me to take a different route to my bus. It seems so silly, and I don't want to go out of my way, but I have learned to trust that prompting and go a different way. If nothing happens, was I safe or silly? I will err on the side of silly.

"We advocate for our kids because we know them, we know ourselves, and we know our family dynamics."

When it comes to making decisions for my kids or getting help for them, I have to know what I know about them. We advocate for our kids because we know them, we know ourselves, and we know our family dynamics. People will say you "should do this or that." And maybe you know it isn't something that will work for your family. TRUST that. Know what you know.

A friend who was blogging suddenly started having some strange things show up in her comments and emails. When she told me about it, I knew she was being stalked. She was trying to downplay the whole thing. But when I asked her, "What do you think is going on?" that was when push came to shove.

She was really bothered because something was off and she knew it. When a co-worker suggested she call the FBI, she did. Then she posted it to her blog and the harassment and crazy emails stopped. Know what you know and always trust your instincts.

Choices

Believe your kids and teach them to trust their instincts too. It's the best way for them to stay safe. Because we are taught *not* to trust our instincts, we tend to minimize what we feel and tell ourselves we're making a big deal out of nothing--overreacting.

There's just enough truth in those messages to cause us to doubt what we know. So, we finally "dis" ourselves. Other people reinforce this self-deprecation. When I started to learn to say, "Thanks, but that isn't going to work for us," or just plain "Thanks," and then did what I believed was right for my family, things ran much more smoothly. Stand by your values. People have tons of advice, but not a lot of listening/hearing skills to match.

I longed for people to listen and hear what I thought was important. I did have friends who believed in me and trusted me to make good choices for my family. I'm so grateful to all who believed in me. What a gift.

How do you know if "what you know" is real or an overreaction? There's a book called *Blink* that can help you better understand this. There were definitely times when I didn't want my kids to do things only because I worried, not because I had a gut feeling. And it's hard letting go as a parent and allowing things to be what they will be. Talk with friends who know and love you. See a counselor or get a coach to help you through those times.

I knew the difference between worry and gut feeling. Sometimes things do happen, even if you didn't have a feeling about them. Don't beat yourself up. You can only do what you can do, and sometimes bad things or tough things lead to great adventures. Looking back in the middle of an adventure doesn't always look like it does in the movies.

When you're in a leadership role, you have to rely on what you know, so start practicing ahead of time if you can. Is there a situation where you're not being true to what you know? What can you do to turn that around? These all feel like trite sayings, but…know what you know. Believe yourself, and stand by what you believe, and this includes your values.

Don't go against your values to do what others think or believe you "should" do. In fact, if you hear a "should" stop and take time to think it through. Is it something that will work for you? If you do it, will it be just because you feel guilty? Will it be because you don't want to let someone down? What "should" you do? I believe that when we are seeking to grow and learn and be "who we be," (being who we were meant to be) that we will know what to do. We will know who to trust, who to take advice from, and most of all, we will make good choices for our families even if it doesn't look like it to others.

Many times you will be misunderstood and disappointed in others who can't support you or believe in you. Sometimes it's incredibly lonely to do what you know is the best for your family. Do it anyway, and remember, this too will pass.

It may be tempting to use your newfound power to manipulate the troops. Resist, and be real and honest, especially with yourself. We all need choices. When we don't believe we have a choice, we become paralyzed.

"...be real and honest, especially with yourself."

When I remarried, I thought I was stuck for life. I didn't want to divorce a second time; I didn't want to feel like a failure. So I tried to make the best of a tough situation – but that made things even worse. But when I realized that I had choices, even though they weren't ones I wanted; I was animated again. When we have choices, then we can take responsibility for staying or leaving. We do not become the victim of no choice.

I tried to give my kids choices as much as possible, because if they made the choice, then they had to take responsibility for it. I had a child who didn't function well when he felt backed into a corner, but when I gave him choices, he felt like he had some control in his life. For example, "You can do it now, or in ten minutes, or you can go stay in your room." Three options, right there!

If you're in a tough situation and feel like there's no way out, look for alternatives anyway. They may not be perfect. You may not want any of them. But just realizing there *are* options is invaluable, having no recourse leads to frustration, victimization, and depression.

I use the option theory in my coaching, parenting, and "friending." Sometimes our friends just need help brainstorming options when they find themselves in difficult situations. Having options increases creativity and possibilities. Noticing options and the ability to help others see their options is a very valuable life skill.

I remember feeling stuck at a job that I hated, marching to the mailbox, and asking myself, "What do I want?" I wanted to know that I would make it. I wanted to know that there were choices and the possibility of a life ahead of me. I didn't want to be a victim of the "this is as good as it gets" message. At that point, I realized if it was meant to be, it was up to me. That's when I began looking at options and my possibilities and made a plan.

It seemed impossible, but impossible was better than staying in a place that was not good or healthy. I hate "I can't because____." How about, "These are my options, but for the time being, I am choosing to stay in this particular situation." Saying it in a way that it is your choice is empowering.

"Having options increases creativity and possibilities."

I don't have an antidote to your life. I can't say that if you do A, B, and C, that life will work. What I am saying is to trust yourself and know what you know. You have a belief system. You have an idea of how life looks, even if it doesn't go the way you planned. Or even if you didn't have a plan, you know if you did, this wasn't it.

Start thinking about your future and plan, what do you want and what do you love? It may take years to get there, but knowing and thinking about a plan while giving yourself grace to get through life is a good place to start.

We know certain things, yet we tell ourselves lies. We tell ourselves we are washed up, and no one will ever love us and all our baggage. We tell ourselves the bad messages we have heard along the way, like, "I will never make it, never amount to anything, or I can't because______." If there is anything I could tell you that might work, it is *change the messages you tell yourself.*

Pay attention to what you're saying in your head. "I messed up again. I can't get anything right." My favorite example is, "I would give anything to have that, or do that." This just causes you to think about what you don't have. When I started to think about what I *said* I would give or do – it stopped me short. Really? No, I *wouldn't* give up my kids to get that car. I wouldn't give "anything" to have that.

Wouldn't you rather think you're making a choice to not have "that" because you wouldn't really give "anything" to attain it? What messages are you telling yourself? Start paying attention to them, and if they're not true, then be big enough to stop them. My teeth are crooked, and I have to fight the message that I'm ugly. I reject that message! Yes, my teeth are crooked - but I've made the choice to leave them this way because I choose other things for my family, rather than paying for braces. It was and still is a choice.

When you take responsibility for what's going through your head, you'll get farther and accomplish far more than if you waste time listening to debilitating messages. Know what you know and take responsibility for it. Do not be the victim of your own story. Yes, things happen that are out of your control. Being abandoned by a husband can leave you victimized. But what will you choose? Will you decide to live in that state or to rise above it? Life is short, and although it doesn't seem like it, your time as a single parent is limited. Before you know it, this too will pass. What will you all remember about your times together?

Make the most of a difficult, sad situation. Validate yourself and give yourself permission to be sad and then move on. Begin rewriting the messages going through your head. They may be yours or they may be from someone else. Don't give them free rent in your head. You can tell yourself new improved messages like, "I am going to get through this," "I am going to find my way," or "I am choosing to ______."

What messages can you reframe and make more positive? Knowing what you know is a broad subject, but the more you get in touch with it, the safer you'll feel safe; and the more you will model this for your children. You know yourself better than anyone, so give yourself permission to make decisions based on what you know to be true for yourself and your family.

Just Wondering:

Are you living with "this is as good as it gets"?

How can you turn that around?

What steps can you take towards, what's next?

What is holding you back?

Do you feel you have a lack of choices?

Are you gripped by fear?

What do you really want?

When have you had a "gut" feeling about something?

How did it turn out?

What can you do to trust your instincts if you don't already?

What is one step?

When have you felt validated?

When have you been able to validate someone else?

What situation are you in that you feel stuck and would like to explore options and choices?

Is there someone safe to do this with?

When have you been in a situation where you thought you had no options?

How did you feel?

What did you do? Did it work out?

Was there someone to blame?

What situation do you find yourself in now where you can create some options?

How about a friend?

Are there people you feel safe to brainstorm with about the choices available to you?

Know What You Know.

7
SUPPORTING THE SINGLE PARENT

Fight the urge to Flee, Fix, and Farm-out

"Next time you put on a dinner, don't just invite friends, invite those who can't return the favor."
- Luke 14:12-14 The Message

Knowing what you know is just one step in this adventure of being a single parent. The single parent has many challenges, and the biggest one is learning to trust yourself and know what you know. So how can others support the single parent?

"The most important thing in supporting a single parent is to believe in them and for them."

The most important thing in supporting a single parent is to believe in them and for them. Believe they will make it. Pity will destroy your relationship with them. Validation will strengthen it. Try not to let your fears overshadow your relationship with the single parent. We (single parents) thrive when friends and family remind us that we are amazing, that we are doing well, and that you are there for us.

When have you felt validated?

What was it like?

When have you been able to validate someone?

What was that like?

We're able to let go of difficult things when we feel validated. We are pioneers just trying to make our way. Actually, there are many who have gone before us, and we want to hear their stories. (My great-grandmother was a single mom. Oh, how I wish I had her journals! How did she make it way back then? What was it like? I could have learned so much from her.)

If you've ever taken a cardiopulmonary resuscitation course, you know there is a certain way to do CPR. We practice on the "Anne" doll, Resusci Anne©. First, you are talking to her to see if she is alert; you check for a pulse, tip her head back, breathe into her, and feel for any breath coming out. Then, you press on her chest to get her heart pumping. No matter how hard you try, you cannot resuscitate Anne. However, if you learn the correct procedures, you can resuscitate a real person. And if you use the correct procedures, you can also resuscitate a single parent.

You can't resuscitate a person without breathing into them. It's the same with a single parent. If you advise, shame, or doubt them, they won't breathe. Encouragement is the breath of life. Pushing on the chest to start the heart is the equivalent of believing in them. Sometimes, once you've resuscitated someone, especially if they were in the water and swallowed some, they may throw up on you! That's just how it works.

Be a good listener who offers no advice unless asked. Just listen to us and hear our hearts. Ask questions like, "How can I support you?" Or even tell us what you're able to do. The hardest thing for us is asking for help, and it's way easier when you prop that door open with a kind offer.

Sometimes we're sad, having a bad day, or struggling with how in the world we'll raise our children, and we need to vent. Sometimes our despair makes you want to rescue--fix us. Just listen and hear. You can offer suggestions with permission like, "May I make a suggestion?" You can offer services like "I could babysit," or "I could drive you or pick up the kids."

"Be a good listener who offers no advice unless asked."

Don't let our anguish overwhelm you. Model for us how to do this; because there will come a time when our children's frustration will overwhelm us, and we will have to listen, hear, validate, and not drown in their despair.

A friend of mine was devastated after she lost her job in a very tough economy. When she finally told her sister, rather than showing compassion and concern, her sister immediately began ordering her to look for a job six hours every day along with various other "duh" tips. She let my friend know that she shouldn't count on her to help. My friend said, "Oh, silly me, I was just looking for a little validation. I thought maybe you would be upset FOR me not at me."

Every situation is different. When a single parent runs into huge challenges, it's scary for everyone. Can you keep a stiff upper lip for us? Resist the urge to fix, and instead, find a way to validate and sympathize. We will get through it. Help us believe in ourselves and fight the doom and gloom. We actually probably already know all the "tips"-- get up daily, look for a job like it is your job, etc. All of that is just common sense. So believe that we have good ideas - brainstorm with us - and encourage us.

Remind us what you know about us. We are creative, resourceful, talented, skilled, and more. Show us it is going to be okay. Walk with us; take us to coffee; just spend time with us. Time is something we don't have much of, so doing projects together is a great way to kill several birds with one stone. We have things that need to be done around the house, so hammer, paint, or vacuum side by side with us.

Be a friend. Stick up for us when you hear family or friends talk about us behind our backs. When others suggest that they know better what's good for us, be our advocate. You can do that well when you've listened to us and know our hearts. Believe in us, even if you don't agree with us. You may want us to do something, anything - move, take a different job, economize. Perhaps you truly believe we're making mistakes, and if we would only listen to you things would be better.

Remember, the single parent is an adult who takes her responsibilities seriously. Trying to force her, or even worse, *shame her* into doing it your way creates a barrier and causes us to close up and think, "I really am alone." When you support and believe in us, we're able to relax and take a short break from pure survival mode and, just maybe, look at things differently.

Let us make our own decisions and use validation to help us. Sometimes you may want us to do things because it's really easier for you. Maybe we make choices to be farther away or work difficult hours, and you think, "How in the world can I help when they're making it so difficult?" Do what you can. Have your own boundaries. Be clear with us about what you are able to do, and how something may be difficult for you. Maybe you will have to tell us you will only be able to baby sit three days rather than five, or not at all, because of the distance.

We love you, too; so take care of yourself. When you overdo it or feel taken advantage of we sense your frustration, believe me. I would rather do it myself than be helped grudgingly. Look for a win-win, but it is not your job to make our lives better. Some of us may try to make you feel guilty, and we might actually succeed for a while. But, we need you to model self-care and boundaries, so we will be able to model it for our kids and take care of ourselves.

Believe in us and hold us big. By "hold us big" I mean be honest with us and believe we can handle a disappointment or a no. Let us struggle because that's when we grow and gain strength. Remember that single parents are doing amazing things all over the world. Help us be great by believing in us. Remind us, "______." Make it something like, "You never give up. You're a great mom. Your kids adore you." Remind us of our greatness because we've forgotten.

Sometimes we have to be in survival mode because of our circumstances, and that can get in the way of our creativity. When my kids' dad left, I went to the welfare office, but they wouldn't help because I said I would be searching for a way to work from home so I could be with my kids. But they wanted proof I was trying for a "real" job. I know my friends and family were thinking I had finally lost my marbles, but they didn't challenge me. I knew how much my kids had already suffered by having their dad move out. And I knew in my heart of hearts that it wasn't the time to leave them. I was also pretty doubtful I could support them on what I could make in a stay-at-home, ground-level new business. But I was stubborn enough to believe I could work it out.

Was that insanity? Possibly, but I believed something would work out and it did. Remember when I got to work in the camp kitchen? The kids were able to have the run of the camp, and I was taken care of in an unbelievable way. My miracle showed up. I had my doubts, but I first had to believe I would find a way to be with my amazing, wonderful children. It paid off. I'm eternally grateful to those who believed in me at that time – their faith in me was a gift.

When I became "needy" -- a divorced mother of three with no job - the first things to go were dignity and choice. I had to ask for help, and some people assume if they help you, they can control you. Isn't that ridiculous? But they often do. That's why I struggled. If you help me, then I will have to do something in return, and my plate is already full. I'm maxed out.

I once saw a great saying on a sign that carried a double message: "When does caring become control?" I took the less obvious meaning: Yeah, do we know when it does become control? What seems like caring to you can be confusing and it can cause a single parent to not ask for help because it's not worth the price. Don't be mistaken - we want the help; we want to give back; but we don't want to be controlled. If you want something in return, ask, don't just tell us. Ask, if what you have to offer is what we need. And if it comes with terms, be upfront.

As hard as this is to say, I must say it. I must stand up for my fellow single parents. Don't give us junk unless we ask for it. Don't give us clothes that are so threadbare you won't wear them. Don't give us couches that smell like pee. We can't afford to get rid of them or pay for the dump. Unless we're mechanics or ask you for a car that doesn't work, don't give us money pit cars. We don't have the time or money to fix them, and we can't afford to have them towed every time they break down. Don't give us outdated food or the less desirable part of the broccoli floret because you won't eat it. Think about our dignity.

Over the course of numerous meetings with people and services for the poor, I've heard comments that I can't even repeat. Everyone has b.s. about being poor, and when I say b.s. I mean belief systems. What are yours? Beggars can't be choosers? Are poor people poor because they don't make good choices? According to whom? How many stories of poverty do you base that on? Or, how about this oldie but goodie, "Once we help them, they will expect more?" That was the farthest thing from the truth in my case. A single parent is grateful for, yet embarrassed by, the help. Most likely she is doing everything in her power to be self-sufficient and even trying to help others.

Many of us need lessons in receiving, because we know it is more blessed to give than receive, and we would love to be on the other end of charity. Treat us with dignity. I remember finally moving from the camper into a house. We had no furniture. I had to give everything away when we moved. Oops, we had no furniture.

"… beggars can't be choosers, right?"

My friend Sue called and said, "I found you a bed at the thrift." I was leery, but hey, beggars can't be choosers, right? When I met with her, she said, "I would never get you a bed from the thrift, but it was still in plastic and was in someone's guest room. It had barely been used." Sue knew how to help while preserving my dignity.

Just remember, as much as you want to help us, it is hard for us to admit we need help. So we may not initially share your excitement. Give us choices, "I have a couch - would you like it? Come look at it and see." Just because we're needy, that doesn't mean we don't want our living room furniture to match.

If you want to buy us groceries, ask what we can use or get a gift card. Kids love macaroni and cheese, right? Not mine. So we had boxes and boxes of macaroni and cheese, because they were inexpensive, people would buy them for us. It was nice, but I gained weight because I loved macaroni and cheese and I was the only one eating it. Also, inexpensive food isn't the healthiest.

Anonymous donations are nice, but sometimes people have a hard time accepting things when they don't know where it came from, especially food. Is it tampered with? One Christmas a woman wanted to take my kids and me grocery shopping at Costco. She wanted us to all go with her so she could see our happy faces while she was buying us much-needed food. I couldn't work it out for all of us to go and it never ended up happening.

I don't mean to sound ungrateful, but I'm just saying how difficult it is for us and hope you will try to understand. I have definitely appreciated all the help I've received. I don't know where I would be without the kindness of others. Now we're in an economy where more and more people need help. It's hard to accept help, to feel helpless, and to feel hopeless. When someone helps out, lends a hand, and treats me with dignity; it is a wonderful gift. Help out if you want to, but don't do it to get praised for being a sensitive person.

You may not get gratitude; you may get frustrated thanks because we hate being needy. Having choices is important and helpful. I remember a woman I was shopping with at the Christmas House

-- a shop where needy folks can buy Christmas gifts for their kids. When she met up with me, she apologized for being late and said, "I had to park down the road." I was surprised she couldn't park closer and she said, "Oh, I parked down the road because I have a fairly new car. I needed a dependable vehicle for work, and I was afraid people would see it and think I didn't really need the help."

I could relate, because when my husband left me for a man, I needed something to help me feel feminine. A friend offered to pay for me to get my nails done and keep them up. I accepted and later was told that someone in my church had mentioned to our pastor that maybe I didn't need help after all, because I seemed to be doing well enough to have my nails done! I stopped getting them done.

I would have loved to have continued, but thought if I was receiving help and people believed I didn't have my priorities straight that I would be judged. I was pretty fragile and didn't want people thinking badly of me. If one person voiced that, how many were thinking it?

Sometimes you will find community where you don't expect it…and you may find that what you thought was your community really isn't. I grew up in a small hamlet where we attended Sunday school. A couple across the lagoon picked us up, along with other neighbor kids, every Sunday morning and took us all to church. My sister and I went faithfully.

I went on to Bible college, then got into radio. My first jobs in radio were at Christian stations, but then I was offered a job at Contemporary Hit Radio Station KIYS in Boise, where I was the morning news and traffic person. I went to a Christian singles retreat the weekend before I started. If any one asked what I did, I told them I worked in radio and was starting at the Number One station in Boise the next week. They were really upset; they voiced that I "should" stay at the Christian station. I didn't tell them I had been fired and that the boss told me I would never make it in radio.

Fast forward past getting married, working with youth, attending Bible study and church, past the divorce, the second marriage with big plans to be missionaries once the kids were grown, to being divorced TWICE. Suddenly, I didn't fit in at church, though church is supposed to be a place where you come as you are. Sundays became very difficult and when the announcements promoted a "dinner for eight" event. Why not seven? Everything seemed to be geared to couples.

It felt as if people at church didn't know what to do with me. The local Catholic church and the Family Resource Center gave us a food basket and signed us up for Christmas services. Those were low times, but no one in my church seemed to know. There were really only a couple of people who were interested in me and my life. When people did ask how things were going, I would just tell them good things. I didn't want to complain, but I longed to connect with people at church.

I wasn't able to go to Bible studies because I couldn't leave my kids with babysitters. They would say, "Oh, just leave them. They'll be fine." But, I knew from experience that I would get a call and have to go back and get them. Then we all felt bad. This was denial, just ignoring our reality with "It'll be fine."

I went back to Bible college to get my degree in social services, thinking I could get a better job with a B.S. (no pun intended) behind my name. I didn't want to tell people I was divorced, let alone twice. So I didn't. And the crazy thing was, no one asked. People weren't really interested in my life. I'm a connector, so I was interested in others; I knew how many kids they had and if they were married. I knew what their internships were and whatever I could learn about them because I was curious. I was worried that I'd have to come up with big distractions to avoid telling my big dark secret, but I didn't have to at all. Moreover, I discovered that this is true almost everywhere.

People often aren't curious. They don't ask. A co-worker was planning to go to a "meet up" event, and she told me she was going to say she worked for a fictitious company doing data entry. She said she was concerned that if she revealed that she worked in radio, people might make a big deal out of it. (Stalkers are a real concern for those working in the media.)

But I suggested she go for it, to tell them what she did and that chances were no one would even ask what station she was on. The next time we worked together, she told how she actually ended up telling the group that she worked in radio - and no one was even interested. She said, "They didn't even ask what station or what time I was on the air."

"I don't mind being "that single mom." I just want community friendship."

I long to be involved in church and fit in, but there's a part of me that doesn't want to deal with the pain of rejection and judgment. I don't want to be "that divorced lady." I don't mind being "that single mom." I just want community friendship. I remember wanting to be connected with my church, and after the second divorce no one there seemed interested in me. In fact, I wondered if some of my church friends even knew I had kids, because they were with their dad on Sundays. Yet the Family Resource Center and the single moms' network knew all about me and loved me.

I would get calls from people with the center for advice or just to talk about their struggles. They weren't afraid of me because I was divorced. They never told me I didn't try hard enough, should have sought godly advice before marrying (which I actually did), or that I made bad choices. They just accepted and loved me. It was really wonderful. I wanted my church to be my community, but in actuality, my community became my church.

There are churches with programs to help single moms, and that's wonderful news. If churches don't know how to help, it's hard to be the one to tell them how to help. But if they're open to it, let your needs be known. Maybe you will be the one to start a program in your church. Or maybe find a church that is known for helping out single parents. The church can't do it all, and that's why I am an advocate for church and community working together to help single parents.

"Check in, validate, and encourage us."

If you have a single parent in your life, it's a great opportunity for you to grow and learn. Believe us, and believe *in* us. Do your best to keep our dignity intact. Don't pawn us off on others. Help us or not; we will figure it out. Validate us and remember to let us have choices. Don't torment us because you're concerned. We have to do what we believe is right for our families. We may even come around to seeing it your way if we feel we have a choice.

There are times when you will want to avoid single parents, because their needs seem so great and the situation seems so bleak. Just remember, you don't have to avoid us. Check in, validate, and encourage us. That's enough. I'm not saying that we're perfect or that we make all the right choices. I'm just saying it is tough and lonely, and when our friends and family become advice-givers rather than supporting us, we start to isolate and back away from the ones we need the most.

Some of us take an attitude of "I'll show them." It's kind of misplaced aggression; it is like saying we won't let anyone know our needs for fear there will be strings attached. We just resolve to go it alone. It's easier to take advice from friends and family when you're totally convinced they love and believe in you. It sounds really shallow to say, but the truth is, I think any of us can hear advice best from someone we know completely accepts us. That happens when we feel validated, heard, and supported. Probably 95 percent of the time it isn't advice we want. We know what to do. We just want to be heard and feel like we're not alone.

Fight the Urge to Flee, Fix and Farm Out

Fight the urge to flee, ignore, and avoid. Fight the urge to fix. Fight the urge to farm out what you cannot do for us. Do what you can do, and don't guilt others into helping. We all have our own convictions of how and where we help or give money. Something we may be passionate about may not be ringing someone else's bell. So if you "force" or guilt them into helping, it's not a pretty picture. I know you feel desperate and want to help. This is a chance for you to discover what you believe about faith. You will get through this, and so will we. This, too, shall pass.

Just Wondering?

How have you supported the single parent in your life?

Is there something different you will try now?

What is it like "not to be able to help"?

Have you had to say no in the past to them?

How did their situation work out?

What is your role in their life?

What can you do to honor their choices when you don't agree with them? Has this happened to you before?

What are ways you have encouraged the single parent in your life?

What are ways you have validated them?

8
Taking Responsibility for What is Mine

The truth will set you free--
but first it will make you miserable.
--from a Raggedy Ann poster.

You have to "own" your part as a friend, parent, or relative of a single parent. Take responsibility for your feelings and find ways to support us without pawning us off, ignoring us, or fixing us. Now, it's time for us to own our part in our lives so we don't live in a state of victimization. I am a Christian; I am divorced twice. Both times I married I was a Christian, walking with God. My husbands were professing Christians.

I have been told that I didn't pray hard enough, that I didn't listen to God. I have been blamed, ignored, and sometimes no longer allowed to work in church because I'm divorced. The church doesn't know what to do with us. I even heard someone say, "You will be more accepted by Christians if you kill someone, go to prison, get out, and go on the speaking tour."

I knew a widowed missionary with four kids. She met a wonderful man who loved God, adored her, and her children. But her church forbade her to marry him because he was divorced. People don't even bother to ask the circumstances. Who divorced whom? Judgment comes strong and swift in words like failure, tarnished, damaged, broken. One friend, when she heard I was separated, told me I should try harder. How? He was gay!

Yes, there are many circumstances for divorce, some more noble than others. Going through my first divorce, I believe that I touched more lives for God because I was honest in my struggles. There are certain "unforgivable" sins - not biblical sins, rather people's notions about what they are uncomfortable with - and we all have our own ideas about what those things are.

A friend of mine whose heart is to help the "good girls" who end up pregnant and on their own tells me that she has discovered that single pregnancy is one of those "sins." The good girl "messed up," made her own bed, and now she has to lie in it - forever marked because she had a baby. And we all know what that means she was doing. She's shamed, disciplined, and sometimes ostracized by church or family because she's the one who "got caught."

Oh, and by the way, she is having the baby. In our society, she should get a medal. It is so easy to just sweep the unborn child away, and it takes as much courage to face the disapproval of those who don't want you to keep it as those who judge you for getting preggo out of wedlock! But we all struggle with our opinions and we all have our stuff.

Another friend whose husband abandoned her was encouraged by some women in her church to never give up on him, so she waited for him to come to his senses while she was living in a shelter, and he was living with his girlfriend. She struggled with despair. I can't help but wonder how come no one in the church she was attending, who were advising her to hang in there, took her in?

Full of advice, but no one offered her what she really needed, which was a safe place to be with her baby girls. It seems the one left behind gets the blame. There is no justice in divorce. It hurts the children, and even our animals suffer. It's not pretty and I certainly don't want to glamorize it. But don't ignore us or blame us.

A friend who I met shortly after my kids' dad left wrote a song about me. It's called "Dancing in the Moment." The first verse was about someone who ended up in prison, confessed, and was free in God even though still imprisoned. The verse about me was "She woke up one morning and her husband was gone, now she's dancing in the moment." She sang it to a friend of hers and was blown away by the comment. "How come her husband left? What did she do?" My friend, in her wit, said, "She wasn't man enough."

When I returned to Bible college to complete my bachelor's degree, I didn't tell people I had been divorced twice. I said I was a single mom and my kids' dad is gay. I chose to be vague because of my fear of being judged. I was more worried about what *I thought* people would think about me, rather than giving them the benefit of the doubt. I felt so much shame from "failing twice" I didn't want to expose myself.

I remember one woman sharing how she had prayed and prayed as a single mom for a man to love her and her kids. Then Mr. Wonderful came along, and they had been happily married for many years. She followed it with "If you just wait on God and pray, He will bring the right person for you."

I couldn't help but wonder how come I prayed, went to church faithfully, read my Bible, and yet marriage number two was still a disaster. So I wrote a paper about how it is so easy to impose our success antidotes on to others, but what works for us doesn't necessarily work for someone else.

That's what I love about God. Jesus healed the blind men in the Bible several different ways. We try to make formulas for life, like, "If you do A, B and C you will: lose weight, stay married, get a job, or meet a man." But it doesn't work that way. We all have paths we walk. Consider telling your story as your own, but not as the end-all formula.

I want to share my experience of how divorce has named me, and blamed me, and kept me small in the world.... I would have loved to have thrived, and although that didn't happen for me at church, it did in the world of social services. Working at Big Brother/Big Sister, listening to hurting women, blessed me. I don't judge. I listen with compassion. In that world, I'm really effective. So the world has become my mission field.

When my first husband left, I thought, "Now is the time to go out and speak. Tell my story." But here's the thing: I would have remained the victim. And people would have loved to jump on the bandwagon with me. How terrible; I was betrayed and hurt. I married for love and life. He married to conceal his shame. However, as easy as it is to look at "what was done to me," it's difficult to name my part in it all. After all, I married him.

We were friends and pals and even in his effort to avoid intimacy, I had my own issues. Sexual abuse in my past made it attractive for me to find someone "safe" like a pal. Bad move. Because in the end, I was hurt, and it was hell letting go and moving on, because I had tolerated so much for so long. What I ultimately feared is exactly what happened: I had to go it alone. He was telling me in every way possible (except with words) that he couldn't love me.

I shared with a small group of women early on in my marriage that my husband didn't love me. They had tons of advice, including wrapping myself in cellophane and meeting him at the door. Now I get why he ran screaming from the house after that; he's gay! How terrifying! But at the time, I translated his behavior as something was wrong with me. The answer: Do more, try harder, be better. We both got counseling. My desire for intimacy increased, and his desire to come out of the closet was stronger.

My boys loved watching the G.I. Joe cartoon and the sign off was always "*And knowing is half the battle.*" What are you willing to own? Acknowledge your truth. It won't kill you; it will set you free.

"Honesty is the first chapter in the book of wisdom."

--Thomas Jefferson

We stayed in the situation because we were scared, loyal, willing to keep the status quo, even though we wanted out. Maybe we stayed because we knew our kids would be safer if we did. We knew what we were doing, somewhere deep inside, and it made sense. We do not have to explain our reasons. But because of them we may isolate or be vague. We knew what we knew and we understood why we were doing it.

What is your truth? It was terrifying and scary and lonely and confusing. I stayed in the same place because I believed I could have more control over what my kids were exposed to if I stayed. I chose to stay after I knew the truth. I didn't tell anyone because I knew what I needed to do for myself. As I acknowledge my part, I am free. It's not about beating ourselves up. It's not about what "I shouldn't have done, said, or been." It is about realizing we don't have to do it anymore. It's about taking care of ourselves, not making the same type of choices again! It's about self-preservation. If I admit my part, then I'm likely to not repeat it.

"What is your truth?"

So many times people remarry, and it's just the same person underneath a new look. Get free. I don't mean leave a relationship. I mean the freedom of admitting the truth to yourself.

After my husband left, I was faced with a reality I didn't like very well - all the things I "couldn't do" because of my husband, all the things I couldn't be because of him, I still wasn't doing, or being, even after he was gone. But he couldn't be my excuse any more. I had to take responsibility for living or not living my dreams, and suddenly there was no more scapegoat. I had to face that I was my own worst enemy. So many times we blame others for what we cannot do or are not willing to try, and we blame them, so we don't have to step out and face our fears.

Being on my own caused me to really look at myself and stop hiding behind others. I was forced to look at my life and what I wanted and to admit I was the only one who was getting in my way. What are you afraid of doing? What goal are you not reaching because you're blaming someone else?

I had to realize no one was going to make good things happen for me. If it is going to be, it's up to me. Of course, there are situations where that does happen and you're sabotaged by a spouse, but that's not what I mean. I'm talking about the situations where facing your biggest desire is too scary, so we stash it behind our "scapegoat" to avoid owning responsibility in it.

How many people let their dreams and desires slip away because they're too afraid? How many would rather dream about something than actually step out and face possible failure? Failure is opportunity. It's disguised as something awful, but we survive failure every day. And the people we're amazed at are the Thomas Edisons of the world, who say things like, "I haven't failed, I just discovered a hundred ways my idea won't work."

We're just looking for the way it will work. Stay with it; don't give up and don't blame others for your dream going awry. It isn't too late to do something you love. It's a process, and maybe part of it is finding the kind of people, friends, or coaches to encourage and support your inner strength. It's there, but you may have forgotten or covered it up. Find it; don't let the world pass you by. You get one life.

"I haven't failed, I just discovered a hundred ways my idea won't work."

I passed up opportunities while I was a single mom because of my values and my situation. I didn't blame my kids. I did what I thought was best for us, and at times, that meant putting a particular dream on hold. But during the wait, I gained so much. Time with your kids can never be replaced. Now, I'm off pursuing another dream with even more tools in my box. I spent the last eight or so years alone single by choice until my kids were raised. I didn't want to put them through any more chaos than they had already experienced. This gave me time to look deeper. Recovery is like an onion - it happens layer by layer.

For a long time, I let the label "divorced" both haunt and define me. But because I was willing to own my stuff, I was able to do the personal work to let it go and love myself. Don't let your scapegoats get in the way of doing your inner work, and don't let someone else's label define you. It can be hard work to love yourself after the trauma of divorce. It's hard work, as a single parent, to accept permission to play, to take care of yourself, or even put yourself first. Particularly as women, these things scream "SELFISH" – but self-care is vitally important life skill. But when you take care of yourself, you are better equipped to take care of others. It actually creates a ripple effect and it is wonderful.

How do you grieve a loss as big as a divorce, the dream to grow old with the one you love and be grandparents together, and still accept and be grateful for the opportunity of becoming stronger, and more whole in the suffering? The reality is that many situations involve suffering. So the question becomes, "Where is the blessing in it, and how can I accept it, even be grateful without betraying myself and the hurt?" It's a journey.

"What doesn't kill you makes you stronger"

Until I got divorced, I never even considered applying the word "ambivalent" to myself, and now it is a theme in my life. According to the dictionary, "ambivalent" means: Uncertainty or fluctuation, especially when caused by inability to make a choice or by a simultaneous desire to say or do two opposite or conflicting things.

There are so many choices that exist side by side in each situation. I am choosing to let this be my journey and to accept what the philosopher Nietzsche once wrote, "What doesn't kill you makes you stronger." I remember thinking, "If this is all about being strong and helping someone else, I am going to be ticked." Life isn't fair. What we make of it is what counts. There were, and still are, days that I feel sorry for myself. There are even days when I have panic attacks, thinking I won't survive. But I do, and now I even thrive.

What I have the most regret about is that while raising my kids I had to deal with so many issues that took my energy away from enjoying them and having fun times to look back on. Believe me, I know my kids will have their issues to deal with. If they ever come to me and say, "Hey, Mom, I am pretty messed up because of my childhood," I hope I'll be able to validate them. I will try my hardest not defend myself. There's no need. Their reality belongs to them, even if I see it differently.

With three kids, each of them will tell a different story of their youth. The best gift I can give them is letting them have their realities by validating and supporting them. My daughter is beginning to tell pieces of her story. She shares parts with me, and then apologizes. I tell her that it is her story to tell, and it is her reality, even if it stings a little. It's okay. She's just trying to make her way and make sense of what happened to her. And the more OKAY I become with myself and my choices, then the easier it becomes to let my kids have their stories.

So in this chapter I am letting go of the victim, and I am taking ownership of my part. It doesn't mean I'm taking all the blame, but I'm also not shifting it. Some of you have horrendous stories, so please don't see this as me minimizing your experiences. I know that some of you have lost your children, or are hiding them. Or, you're staying because your children may be safer if you stay until they're grown. I would never dismiss abuse. It is real, and I trust you will deal with it. If you need to get away, there are safe houses.

It bears repeating: I want to be careful when I tell my story not to minimize anyone else's. Fear of being minimized was what kept me silent for so long. I don't want my story to be seen as a formula for life. It's my story of how I dealt with my situation, and it is very different from your story. If I could give advice, it would be to know what you know, trust your instincts, and remember that this, too, will pass. There will come a day when things are different. Don't beat yourself up. Do what you know is right for your family. Don't let others bully you into doing something you aren't ready or prepared to do. Trust your instincts. Get help if you need it. And by all means, tell your story.

There are others in your situation who need hope that you can offer. The truth is that when we struggle together, we have hope. Struggling in isolation puts us in danger of losing hope, vision, and dreams. I can't tell you why I divorced twice and other friends are married twenty or thirty years. A friend from Bible college told me I didn't pray hard enough before I said, "I do." Others have said...the signs were there and I should have known.

I've spent hours in the whys and it gets me nowhere. Here's what I do know. I have three amazing children who I cannot imagine being without in this world. I have learned some incredible things through the marriages. Although both times I thought I was getting married for life, it just didn't work out that way. I am here today. I am a mom. I am a professional. I am experiencing the empty nest. And I am watching my kids accomplish awesome things.

"I am here today. I am a mom. I am a professional. I am experiencing the empty nest. And I am watching my kids accomplish awesome things."

We did not come through untouched. Each of them has a story - a very different one from mine and their siblings. It's just life! We can't keep ourselves safe from everything life can throw.

We can't predict the future. There are no guarantees, but no matter what our "lot" is, it's easier when shared with community.

We are where we are, and the next step is forward. The next step may be now, or it may be after a while, a rest, a nap, or when a child is raised. The point is, there can be a next step, and it starts with you believing in yourself. Remember to breathe. When things get so overwhelming, go back to the basics. Breathe; take a nap; tell yourself in no uncertain terms that you are going to make it.

"Breathe. Take a nap."

There's so much to learn from horses. (I've been around them my whole life, and I love them.) When you're training a horse and they have a meltdown and don't know what to do - they don't do a pattern right or forget what to do - you take them back to the basics and walk through the steps again. Here is a halter; this is how we walk; that is what we have to do for ourselves.

When things get to be too much, go back to the basics. Reduce it to the ridiculous and you will find one thing you can do. Breathe. Take a nap. Remember to look for things you are grateful for in the moment while you're breathing or floating off into a nap; gratitude is life.

Take the time to acknowledge and accept your part in your situation. It's not about blame; it's about freedom. It is also a gift to your children. When we live blaming the other parent, it is not healthy for anyone. It may even be that you stayed too long trying to honor your vows, but in an unhealthy way.

Find what is yours and own it. It may be as simple as recognizing that you married someone with a mental illness or deeper problem. It's not blame; it's finding your reality. It is not our job to "diagnose," but there are people, adults, or perhaps ex-spouses with fetal alcohol syndrome, and they can't take responsibility in the way we want them to. You find yourself saying. "Is it to much to ask them to ___ (fill in the blank)?" Sometimes the answer is "Yes."

Know what you know and do your part. There are ex-spouses who have borderline personality disorder and are not diagnosed. (There are books on the subject, like *Quit Walking on Eggshells.)* They don't have the same rationality that most people have, and so, yes, they will cause trouble, but find your part in it.

Get educated, read the books, and find out how you can get on with your life, even if they have serious issues, and especially if it's your kids' parent. This isn't a formula to use so life will be great. It's a suggestion to find where you fit in and find a way to live without being the victim of the parent of your children. Sometimes it takes extreme measures. Get support and help and do your part. Learn, grow, and live the adventure.

Just Wondering:

Not to victim-blame or negate betrayal, devastation, hurt, or abuse, but what is yours?

What part can you own?

For me, I put all the "stuff" on the shelf where I can still see it and know it was real....My husband was gay. Now what can I say is true about me? I needed someone safe.

What can you own about your situation?

With all judgment aside, what do you know about yourself and your situation? What are you choosing?

I chose to live with a secret. Maybe I would do it again. What can you own about your choices?

> ***"What is your truth... what can you own up to?"***

Now it's your turn. I needed____________Or I turned to someone to replay my past, my family...__________I tolerated____________________________________. No explanation of why...I just tolerated...neglect...being unloved _________I put up with______________. It's okay....No one is judging you...and your inner critic can just sit this one out.

How about, "I always knew ___________________."

What is your truth... what can you own up to?

Own your values. They are what you live your life by, even if you haven't named them. Here is a list of values:

Abundance
Acceptance
Accomplishment
Accountability
Achievement
Acknowledgement
Activeness
Adaptability
Adventure
Affection
Affluence
Alertness
Altruism
Amazement
Ambition
Amusement
Appreciation
Approachability
Approval
Articulacy
Artistry
Assertiveness
Assurance
Audacity
Awareness
Balance
Being the best
Belonging
Benevolence
Boldness
Bravery
Brilliance
Calmness
Camaraderie
Capability
Carefulness
Celebrity
Certainty
Challenge
Change
Charity
Charm
Chastity
Cheerfulness
Clarity
Closeness
Comfort
Commitment
Community
Compassion
Competence
Competition
Concentration
Confidence
Connection
Conservation
Consistency
Contentment
Continuity
Contribution
Conviction
Cordiality
Courage
Courtesy
Craftiness
Creativity
Credibility
Curiosity
Daring
Decisiveness
Delight
Dependability
Depth
Desire
Determination
Devotion
Dexterity
Dignity
Diligence
Direction
Discipline
Discovery
Diversity
Dreaming
Drive
Ease
Education
Effectiveness
Efficiency
Elegance
Empathy
Encouragement
Endurance
Enthusiasm
Environmentalism
Ethics
Excellence
Excitement
Experience

Expertise
Exploration
Expressiveness
Extravagance
Fairness
Faith
Fame
Family
Fashion
Fearlessness
Fidelity
Fierceness
Financial independence
Fitness
Flexibility
Focus
Fortitude
Frankness
Freedom
Friendliness
Frugality
Fun
Gallantry
Generosity
Giving
Grace
Gratitude
Growth
Happiness
Harmony
Health
Helpfulness
Heroism
Holiness
Honesty
Honor
Hopefulness
Hospitality
Humility
Imagination
Impact
Impartiality
Independence
Influence
Ingenuity
Insightfulness
Inspiration
Integrity
Intellect
Intelligence
Intensity
Intimacy
Introspection
Intuition
Intuitiveness
Inventiveness
Investing
Involvement
Joy
Justice
Kindness
Knowledge
Leadership
Learning
Liberty
Lightness
Liveliness
Logic
Longevity
Love
Loyalty
Making a difference
Marriage
Meaning
Meekness
Mindfulness
Modesty
Motivation
Mysteriousness
Nature
Neatness
Nerve
Noncomformity
Obedience
Open-mindedness
Openness
Optimism
Order
Organization
Originality
Outdoors
Outlandishness
Outrageousness
Partnership
Patience
Passion
Peace

Perceptiveness
Perfection
Perkiness
Perseverance
Persistence
Persuasiveness
Playfulness
Pleasantness
Pleasure
Poise
Popularity
Power
Practicality
Pragmatism
Pride
Privacy
Proactivity
Professionalism
Prosperity
Prudence
Punctuality
Purity
Rationality
Realism
Reason
Reasonableness
Recreation
Reflection
Relaxation
Reliability
Relief
Reputation
Resilience
Resolve
Resourcefulness
Respect
Responsibility
Reverence
Richness
Sacredness
Sacrifice
Saintliness
Satisfaction
Science
Security
Self-control
Selflessness
Self-reliance
Self-respect
Sensitivity
Sensuality
Serenity
Service
Sexiness
Sexuality
Sharing
Shrewdness
Significance
Silliness
Simplicity
Sincerity
Skillfulness
Solidarity
Solitude
Sophistication
Spirit
Spirituality
Spontaneity
Spunk
Stability
Status
Stealth
Stillness
Strength
Structure
Success
Support
Surprise
Sympathy
Synergy
Teaching
Teamwork
Temperance
Thankfulness
Thoughtfulness
Thrift
Tidiness
Timeliness
Traditionalism
Tranquility
Trust
Trustworthiness
Truth
Understanding
Unflappability
Uniqueness
Unity
Usefulness
Variety

Victory
Virtue
Vision
Vitality
Volunteering
Warmheartedness
Warmth
Watchfulness
Wealth
Willfulness
Willingness
Winning
Wisdom
Wittiness
Wonder
Worthiness
Youthfulness
Zeal

Pick your top ten:

1

2

3

4

5

6

7

8

9

10

Prioritize them:

1

2

3

4

5

6

7

8

9

10

How do they match up with how you're living?

What are the values you are living by?

Look at your life. How are your values playing out?

What is number one on your list?

How is it playing out in your life?

Is it number one in the way you live?

Now that you're looking at the completed list, is number one on the list still number one?

Does it match up?

Do you want to keep it number one?

If it doesn't match up... what steps can you take to make your life and your values align?

This is something to think about and discuss with safe people.

9
Resuscitating the Dream

"Dreams are necessary to life."
--Anais Nin

"You may not be able to describe it. You may have forgotten it. You may even no longer believe in it. But it's there."
--Bruce Wilkerson

This adventure we're living takes all kinds of twists and turns. When I did the hard work of admitting and acknowledging what was "mine" and taking responsibility for it, I found some peace.

It seems like that was when I started remembering my dream. What was my dream exactly? I wasn't sure. I knew what I loved, but I didn't know how it would all come together. I did hope for a coaching radio show, but it seemed impossible. I had clients who were on their way and living their dreams. So I kept thinking, "My time will come."

I didn't realize, at the time that I was doing other things, I was taking steps toward it. You may have a dream that has died or been buried - one that you let go of long ago because life happened. Maybe you never had a dream; you didn't have a chance to even think about that. Maybe you can't remember it or are living in such survival mode that you can't even think about it.

Maybe you're angry at how your life is going and that there is never enough, and that people have to help with food and rent. Maybe you are wondering where God is in all this struggling.

I don't have the answer to that; I do know that my faith has been challenged and sometimes my prayers seem unanswered. I know what it is to feel forgotten, overlooked, and invisible. It can feel like fighting a war all by yourself and no one, including God, cares. I've been there.

"Maybe you are wondering where God is in all this struggling."

I yelled at God, but He didn't yell back. I thought if I lived right, things would be good.. But here I am, struggling to make ends meet, working more hours a week than I can handle, nothing seeming to be getting better, and you're asking me to resuscitate my dream? I know it's tough, and maybe you need a little more time.

Maybe you walked away from a job you loved because you had to make more money to raise a family. Maybe you had to take a time out from school because life demands you work 60 hours a week. And now on top of that, I'm supposed to think about what I love, what I want, and what will make me happy?

It feels like a joke. I don't want any more heartache. To remember, discover, or resuscitate a dream is a luxury I can't afford and a potential heartache I don't want. It all seems impossible, and I don't have the energy for any of it.

Just remember, breathe and start small, because this is your opportunity. What if you could do anything and you knew you wouldn't fail? This is your chance to begin to wonder about what's next. Maybe it's what you're doing now. So are you passionate about it? I dare you to take the time to breathe new life into an old dream or discover a new one.

I've asked many people what they love and what they want to do when they grow up, even if they are grownups. And more times than I can count, people have said, "I don't dare think about that!" That is shocking to me. But, it's scary to think about what you love and what could be.

It takes a brave soul to step into such unknowns. I don't know where the path will lead, but I do know that when you get in touch with what you love, it brings hope, wonder, and joy. It gives us the fuel to keep going. It reminds us we have a purpose.

It reminded me that there was Someone bigger than me with better plans than I and that I could do more than just survive--by stirring my passion I could thrive.

I dare you to discover or resuscitate your desires, dreams, and passions! What do you love? In my workshops, I ask you to take one minute and say out loud what you love. I love this activity, and people close to me have gotten very good at this. What I discovered is stressed out moms with huge burdens can't do it. It takes some coaching to remind them of what they love.

"I dare you to discover or resuscitate your desires, dreams, and passions!"

Take one minute; say or write (I'm a huge journal or blog advocate) what you love. Reviving the dream begins with getting in touch with what you love. What do you love? How can you get back in touch with what you love?

I love the beach, my family, gardening, dogs, cats, horses, creating things, hanging out with friends, reading books, and the list goes on and on. This activity may seem silly. But when I began to get in touch with what I loved and began nurturing my soul, my family benefited.

Do it for yourself; do it for your relationship with others. What do you love? Make this a daily activity along with what you are grateful for, try writing or saying five of each, each day. Do it in the shower, the car, with your morning coffee. Make it a routine and see what happens.

In the book *Simple Abundance*, author Sara Ban Breathnatch talks about creating a room or a space to "be" a place that is just for you to write, think, paint, play music, or do whatever soothes your soul. My kids inherited a rocking chair from their great gram. We put it in front of the wood stove and it became "my place" in the mornings before they got up. I'm a morning person, so I would get up early with my book, Bible, journal, and coffee. I read and journaled for as long as possible in the place that was mine.

In the spring, the rocker was moved from the wood stove to the window, where I could see the garden and the valley. Funny thing about the rocker - it tipped over a lot. Like the time I went to sit in it with my breakfast and Dusty, the cat, decided to sit in it at the same time - we all went tumbling over. In fact, as a joke we would tip it over so when someone walked in the door they would think one of us had fallen over in the chair. We all need a place like a corner that says "me." "This is my place."

What are some ideas for a place for you? Do you already have one? How often do you hang out there? If you don't already have a "place," what are some ideas for creating a space? Where might you go for some solitude, even for five or ten minutes a day?

Later, I moved to my BED. My sister bought me an electric blanket and a beautiful bed in a bag set. My house was COLD in the winter, and being under an electric blanket was a bit of heaven. I spent the fall and winter in bed doing my personal reading, and then when I started college, it became my office. I was warm and cozy. I had a laptop and was able to do homework in the comfort of my beautiful bed.

In the spring, it was back to the window overlooking the garden. I found comfort and rest in a place that felt like home. When everything around me seemed to be awry I had a place to get centered. When we find our place and think about what we are grateful for, we rediscover what we love. Our hope begins to revive. Our creative juices start flowing and we get a nudging of possibilities. That is when it becomes safe to wonder what's next.

One friend turned her camper into her "art studio." We made curtains and everything! Another friend created her living room in all her favorite colors and found the perfect chair to make her "spot." A client turned one corner of her tiny living room into a music studio, with music on the walls and instruments all around - to her it was heaven.

Where is your "spot?" It doesn't have to be a room, just a corner, or a chair. Where is your space? Don't have one? Awesome! How fun to begin to discover your place! Find it and be in it. And practice the gratitude exercise... five things you're grateful for, and five things you love. Do it every day and see how your perspective shifts.

Count on the "gremlins" to start their mocking. Get used to it. That said, make friends with those gremlins, because they're here to stay. They don't go away. In fact, the closer you get to your dream, the more gremlins will try to destroy you.

Just know that the creative voices can speak much louder than any gremlins. They can actually take over so it's hard to hear them. I can say that with all honesty. As I write this book, the gremlins scream at me, "This will never happen!

What do you have to say to anyone? Look at your life! It's a mess! And you're in debt!" The gremlins stir up my shame. I can't bear the shame, but I can bear the reality of it.

As I continue to dig my way out of debt, it's easy to feel like a failure – until I remember that I'm in this because of the struggle of single parenting. And I'm not alone! Lots of us are struggling with the same issues. So when I feel like I want to go hide in a cave, that's when it's important to remember that overcoming is all about staying connected with community. Then, the shame seems a lot less shameful.

"Stick with it. Focus on what you love. Do not give in to the gremlin."

Today, I'm finding a way to make the feeling of failure spur me to make things happen. I keep plugging away at my dream and believe with all my heart that I have what it takes to get there.

It doesn't mean it will be easy or that it will happen overnight. It's NEVER easy. If it were, we'd all be doing it. Stick with it. Focus on what you love. Do not give in to the gremlin. Resist the gremlin speak positive true statements write them down so you have them when the haunting starts.

I am....

Creative,

Funny,

Responsible.

Ask friends to give you words about you and your character. These words will be your ammunition against the gremlins. The gremlin's job is to find what you love and destroy it. I don't know why... but we all have that voice that says, "Who are you to think you can ________?" (Fill in the blank with your goal or dream.)

"A bird doesn't sing because it has an answer,
it sings because it has a song."
--Lou Holtz

Remember when I started thinking about hosting a coaching radio show. I wouldn't tell anyone for the longest time - and when I finally did tell two friends, I whispered it. I was embarrassed, because making it happen seemed impossible and silly.

"It takes a lot of courage to show your dreams to someone else."
--Erma Bombeck

I started thinking about the show anyway and ruminated over the possibilities. I started listening to other "coaching shows." I didn't think they were as good as my idea. I had this crazy dream, and I didn't know how, but I started to think I could pull it off. I asked myself what it would take. What is one step? So I thought, well, I could make a demo tape.

Now, I worked in radio. I know how to do a demo. It was GREAT fun. When I look back it seems silly, but what happened was I sent it out and a disc jockey friend invited me to be on his show for New Year's Day to talk about resolutions. It sounded fun, but I was so scared. Still, it gave me the opportunity to make a new demo and the excitement of the adventure made the dream seem more possible.

"Be a rock star."

In the beginning, when you have a dream you have to go completely on believing in the impossible or at least what seems highly unlikely, but then as it actually begins to happen, you feel stronger and stronger. What would you do if you could do anything? Don't think. Just say it...blurt it out...write it down.

I'll never forget meeting with a colleague who I was on the air with, but had never met in person. I admired her work and thought it would be good to get to know her, so we went out to breakfast. In the midst of our conversation, I asked her, "What would you be if you could be anything you wanted?" I'll never forget her answer: "Be a rock star." At first, I thought she was joking. But she wasn't. And putting her dream into words and saying it did something.

Within a few months, she was in a band playing her saxophone, dressing the part, and doing amazingly. Not only that, the gigs her band played were fundraising events, and there were TONS of really famous musicians who gave of their time and talents to raise money. She was a rock star!

It is so fun for us to reminisce now. We talk about the day in the cafe after we had both finished an overnight shift with lack of sleep and sanity, and how our lives have changed since then because we both had a dream. What would you do? Say it now. Write it down! Don't edit yourself. "I can't because it is not allowed." Speak the impossible dream.

After you say it or write it…start to dream...not just think. Dream about it. Picture yourself doing "it." Find pictures you can cut out to make a collage of what it will be like when you're living your dream. When you begin dreaming again, find a way to reduce your plan to the ridiculous. Do what I like to call "toe mopping" (to be explained later) your way to the next step.

"Don't edit yourself."

Sometimes the big picture is overwhelming. Still, the truth is you *can* do it. The "it" may change shape as you move toward it. But don't stop. Even if it is months between steps, don't ever stop. It's okay that there are stops and starts. Do what you need to, but don't let go of hope and wonder.

Don't Stop Believing

Hope and wonder are life. That's is how I made it on those days when I wanted to give up. Wonder what's next: I wonder how your dream will play out. Belief, hope, and wonder are what drive our purpose. We are here for a purpose.

It is not about the "size" of the purpose. Put simply, we are here to do something and to be somebody. Being who we are and sharing our journey is part of the purpose. What is your purpose?

There are so many books out there to help you determine that goal - how-to books and others with formulas that say: "Do this and that and your dreams will come true!" They provide antidotes and formulas to get you to your dream. One title that really sounded attractive to me: *Ninety Days to Living Your Dream*. Boy, how I wanted to do that because it sounded like a quick formula to success. But we have to know what we know and do what we can do in our own time frame.

"We are here for a purpose."

"Thirty Days to a New You," or "Sixty Days to Having the Life You Love," sounds attractive, but unrealistic. It's about your timing and no one else's. I'm not saying the fast track doesn't work for some. But it doesn't work for all of us. If you're one for whom it doesn't work, then welcome to my world! For me, it was more like fifteen to twenty years to living your dream in the midst of *life*. I used to say, "When life gets in the way," but really, it's in the midst of the process of life.

When I was 30, this was not the book I would have even considered writing. When I was a newlywed, writing a book on survival as a single parent would have been the farthest thing from my mind - I was going to be married forever. It was probably a good thing I didn't get to my dreams in three months back then!

I don't want all the same things now that I did in my twenties, although some things have been constant. One constant is a love for communicating through radio. I always wanted to be in radio, but it seemed to become a vehicle for my dreams when I had the idea to do a call-in coaching program that would help people.

Coaching can be expensive so this was a way I could do what I loved and give back. It all seemed so simple at first, but I was soon brought back down to earth. When I started sending out demos and pitching the program proposal, I didn't get any responses. But I kept putting myself out there, and although it hurt, I got back up and tried again.

Eventually, doors opened, even when they were dollhouse-size doors. Things happened, slowly but surely. It wasn't easy; it was hard work and sacrifice, but I was on my way doing what I loved and it didn't seem like work. Even though I was never interested in doing traffic or news, that's where I ended up when I got into radio. I got a job with Westwood One Metro Networks (now Total Traffic). We contract news and traffic to radio stations nationwide.

In Seattle, we did traffic in Utah, Spokane, Portland, and Seattle. I was fortunate to be on many Seattle and Spokane stations. I learned to write news, and it improved my writing skills. I bartered for voice lessons with my friend, Janine, who usually worked with people who wanted to sing. With her help, I improved my breathing and other essentials that helped me develop my radio voice.

Neither writing nor voice lessons were in my original plan, but both opened doors that would not have opened otherwise. Under all the pain and struggles it is there: your passion, your purpose, your loves, your desires. But you need help - maybe not a voice coach or English teacher, but someone in the wings waiting to help.

I noticed my friends and acquaintances needed the same thing I needed: someone to relate to and someone to grab their hand and say: "Together...we can do this together....I will help you when you struggle, and allow you to help me when I struggle."

"Together...we can do this together."

Dreaming is a step-by-step process. If we went from the dreaming to the doing too quickly, we could easily be overwhelmed and knocked off balance. This is why we need roadblocks and obstacles. They have such a negative feel to them, but they actually keep us on track if we use them for what they were intended: Mapping the journey.

Too many people say, "Well, something happened that got in the way, and I took it as a sign not to do it." NO NO NO NO NO NO NO NO NO NO! It is not necessarily a sign.... It is a *lesson*, a turn in the path, an essential element to the journey. Who said it was supposed to be easy? If it were easy, would it be a worthwhile journey? Journeys to the greatest dreams encounter ponderous challenges. For this very reason, roadblocks, obstacles, and struggles are necessary.

The other night, I faced a roadblock. In the past, it would have just about shut me down. But now I see it as a tool. What will I do with this? Will I shove it down? Bowl over it? Pretend it isn't there? No! I will look at the reality of it. How can I use it to get to the "next"? This particular type of block tapped into my greatest fears and made me feel like my dream would never happen. But then I remembered the reality:

I AM in RADIO.

I AM speaking.

I AM diligently working toward my goals and dreams.

All these things are in progress. There are too many positives and too much momentum to stop me from continuing to move toward my dreams. For example, I constantly struggle with the urge to get a second job. I have debts to pay and sometimes they overwhelm me. But the quick fix is not always the answer. Fight the urge to abandon ship and settle for the quick fix.

"Belief versus Reality.... How do we reconcile the two?"

My coach, Patrick Snow, says, "Keep your day job, and use it to provide seed money to fuel the dream." I keep thinking, "There is never any extra for the dream." But I have a network of people who believe in me, some of them even more than I believe in myself, and their words and support keep me going. Their encouragement gives me the guts to wonder, rather than bail, and abandon the dream. It is the "stick-to-it-iveness." Hang on with everything in you. Remember to believe. Remember to wonder. Belief versus Reality....How do we reconcile the two?

"Faith is taking the first step even when you don't see the whole staircase."
--Martin Luther King, Jr.

So many people on their dream paths give it all up to work an unrelated job or do something just for survival. Some panic. I can't tell anyone what they ought to do. Each one has to search his or her heart and to be at peace. It's not easy.

Think of Frodo from *The Lord of the Rings*. His mission was extremely difficult. Along the journey, friends came and went, and people he trusted let him down. When he couldn't go on any longer, his best friend and companion for the journey, Sam, carried him. He stuck to his mission though, and with the unanticipated help of a supportive friend, somehow reached the goal.

We can find a life that is adequate, or we can strive for a dream, which is great. Despite the obstacles, we can, with a little help from our friends, realize our purpose. Why are you here? What feeds your soul? Will you stay on the path, or give up the dream because it seems impossible?

Here's the deal. Even if you give up the dream for whatever reason, like to make more money or to get another job, there will come a time to revive the dream again. It's never too late, and you are never too old. You have been given a lifetime to journey toward your dream. Some are fortunate enough to find it early and make it happen and have a long run of it. Some of us get waylaid and have to finally revive it later, or, like me, revive the latent dream over and over again.

"Why are you here? What feeds your soul?"

So if you decide you have to step away from it, don't bury it. Don't say, "This is the end; it's over." Just know that something in you will stir again and get you on the path. Keep the candle burning and keep the dream alive. Don't let the lie in be-LIE-ve distract you. One lie is that you will never get there. The fun is in the journey, but there are also rough spots that can really bring you down and sometimes set you back.

Believe anyway. Ask those who trust you for encouragement and find a way to believe or re-believe in yourself. *Who* are you? Not what do you do.... *Who* are you? If you aren't sure, go back to "what do you love?" Who you "BE" which is very different from what you "DO." In fact, when you get in touch with who you BE, then you can let go of some of what you DO. Don't let what you do define you. Let "who you be" define you, because what you then do will consistently emerge from within you. So who are you? Still struggling? Then revisit your values and put them together with what you love.

When in your life have you been truly happy? I have a theory that whatever is in your head must come out by word, whether written or spoken. When your thoughts are expressed your brain can process them, but when your thoughts are floating around in your head they are "free falling." They need you to say or write them to give them meaning. So, when in your life have you been truly happy? What is your dream? Sorry to resort to so much repetition, but if you're like me, you will read the question and move on. Try to answer it. I dare you; no I double-dog dare you to say your dream! Don't edit. Just say it. No BUTS.

Maybe what you love or would love to do or be doesn't seem significant enough, or it's too big. Silence the inner critic who intrudes on your dream time. Send it out for ice cream and just be with yourself. See yourself doing it. Trying to justify the inner critic only takes away from the constructive process.

Remember: when I wanted to be a disc jockey and get into radio it seemed absurd in part because there were no women jocks. But that all changed by the time I was ready to be in radio. I didn't even have to be the pioneer!

Dream the impossible dream. Little ideas become the hands and feet that move you toward the dream. So read, subscribe to magazines, make collages, take a trip, get a mentor, volunteer, get an internship, take a class, take any step.... Put it into motion. See what happens. All you have to do is find a way to begin. Believe in yourself; dare to wonder.

"Faith is to believe what you do not see; the reward of this faith is to see what you believe."
--Saint Augustine

No one will take the first step for you. You may feel very alone in the beginning of your journey, but be assured you'll make new friends along the way. People with similar dreams will encourage you despite the curmudgeons who will continue to give poor advice. Have you heard people say something like,

"I don't dare hope because disappointment is too hard?" Forget that idea. Disappointment is hard, but not a killer. In fact, it is a refining fire for your dreams. Trade hope for wonder and dare to wonder the impossible.

"Try again. Dream/hope/wonder--no risk, no disappointment - how sad."

Dream big, and when disappointment comes, well, then have yourself a pity party with your favorite friend and some goodies, and then get back to the dream. Try again. Dream/hope/wonder--no risk, no disappointment - how sad. Don't let the epitaph on your tombstone read: "Played it safe." Take risks and be willing to feel hurt. Pain can be good. Yes, it's hard, but it motivates like nothing else.

Pain can be GOOD.

Take a step.

Risk.

I dare you.

No! I double dog dare you.

You can do it. And you know it. You want someone to believe it for you? I believe it for you.

Imagine it.

Visualize it.

Don't let the dream die.

Revive it.

Nurture it.

There is no time limit.

It is yours; just keep it alive.

Start a dream support group. Get like-minded people to meet with you weekly, and the members of the group can help each other move forward. Find friends who can remind you that your now does not have to be "as good as it gets." If it is good now, IMAGINE what great will be like! We all love stories of people who never give up and accomplish their dreams.

Be the story.

Be the voice for others like you.

You are a pioneer - pave the way.

Be the one to give others hope.

Be the *voice.*

I choose to be the voice. I desperately wanted to hear a voice, someone saying, "This may seem like the end of your dream, but this isn't it. This isn't the end at all." I wanted to believe I could live life doing what I loved, but it seemed so impossible.

I decided I have to pursue my dream; I have to show it can be done not only for myself, but also for other single parents who are putting up with crappy jobs they hate, or well-paying jobs that are accompanied by bad situations and strained relationships. Was I able to reach my goal overnight? No! It took small steps for years, but each increment was fun and set the stage for "what's next." If you want a step-by-step plan, thereare books to help with almost every pecific dream. There are also a multitude of other resources. You can hire a coach, but remember it starts with you.

When I was thinking about a radio coaching show, I made it happen. It didn't turn out as I envisioned. I thought a station would come to me and say, "We would love to have you do a show!" What I discovered is that with the advent of the internet, radio is rapidly changing.

It turned out I had to find my own sponsors. I did get some sponsors, but it would be more accurate to say they found *me.* With the help of some good friends, I pulled it off. I created the show and loved doing it, but when the economy crashed, some sponsors went away and I had to let it go.

I was encouraged to fight for the show, but I still had my day job, parenting responsibilities, and the need to sleep, so I pulled the plug. It hurt like crazy, and my heart was broken. Looking back though, I'm glad the show ended. I realized that as much as I loved it, it wasn't what I was hoping for. Then I had a chance to do it again; it was very different and fun. In the meantime, I keep moving in the direction of my dream while I keep my day job, which I love.

That's not to say the journey hasn't been without a ton of disappointment and frustration. But I'm still going strong. I have my days of self-pity, but I'm looking at obstacles differently now and their challenge almost makes me giddy.

Bring it on!
Be disappointed.
Expect it.
Plan your very first pity party.
Who will you invite?
Will it be a dress up party with hats, goodies, or gifts?
Maybe you could ask a friend to plan it for you.
We all have a friend that loves to plan a party.
Ah dang, it happens, so make the best of it.

Just Wondering:

We all need a place that says "me," and "this is my place." What are some ideas for a place for you?

Where might you go for some solitude, even for five or ten minutes a day? Rediscover what you love and what you are grateful for. What do you love?

What is your dream?

What would you do if you knew you couldn't fail?

What is keeping you from taking steps toward your dream?

What are your gremlins saying?

Will you let them win?

Gremlins need a "Smack Down."
What risk will you take?

10
Choosing your Battles

"The art of living lies in a fine mingling of letting go and holding on."
--Henry Ellis

When you are living in *possibilities* rather than in a defeating place of hating what you do and hating your job, and when you start to look toward and wonder about the future rather than dreading it, you can handle more. You will have more energy for and insight into your daily life. Wondering about the possibilities stirs the dream. Thinking about the dream empowers your life, your thoughts, and your coping skills.

Choose your battles. This is a profound thought in many of life's arenas, and yet very difficult to follow through on. What does it mean? It means balance. It's choosing what is important for you to deal with or "fight" and what you can let go. Simplify your life by choosing what you want to tackle and pass by the lesser things.

Keep it simple.

What's important?

How do I "choose" my battles? How do I know what's going to really matter in the long run and where I should invest my energies? During tough times, you only had so much capacity, so decide what's worth the extra effort. If you're a compulsive cleaner, then a spotless kitchen might mean everything to you.

What is important enough to put energy into that will make you feel better, and what will drain you of what little energy you have left for your family? Is it worth quibbling over table manners with your kids? Is it better to teach them chores versus doing it yourself? When we're raising kids alone, we have to weigh all the things that seem so important. What matters most to you? Have you thought through what you can live with and what you can't live with? Find out what is the most important to you and focus your energies there. Find ways to let the less important things go.

Some people work very hard teaching their children how to clean and others say, "I just don't have the time, it is easier for me to do it myself." Some people will think what you have let go is of supreme importance. They may even try to "should" on you. But you can only do so much and teach so much. If someone else wants to take on the chore, and teach your kids something you don't have time for, then great - as long as you're OK with it. The beauty in choosing is – YOU get to do it!

Another single mom was telling me she expects her kids to strip their beds every Saturday. It really matters to her that their bedding is washed. Well, her busy high school aged kids don't see clean sheets as a priority, and they don't seem to get around to it. This mom shyly told me, "I just do it myself, it is easier and it gets done." I said, "Good for you. But - true confession time – I'm not above bribing my kids."

Her eyes brightened as I told her that before I had kids I was appalled at anyone who would bribe a child to do something they "should" do. After so many years as a single mom, I learned if it was important to me but not to them, I offered a reward when I needed their help. I offered pizza in exchange for a clean house. I made sure the bribe fit into what I needed: If you go to the store for me and get what I need, you can keep whatever change is left over. Hey, sometimes we just have to settle for whatever works and go for it. I can't do it all, teach it all, or manage it all, so I had to let go of what I could, bribe what I couldn't, and find a way to let it be. Not only did I offer myself a little grace, but I also gave my kids a break in the process because they can't do it all either.

I had to learn to choose my battles

In my family, we have quite a collection of disorders. Start with me. I struggle with depression, and I take antidepressants. Believe me; I have heard the whole gamut of opinions about taking them. Others say, "You should just pray harder, try harder, change your diet, do these exercises, and/or think positive thoughts." (Remember, I am a coach and we are all about looking for the positive.) There are some people, motivational thinkers, who say when I am living the life I love, I won't need these pills anymore. I know what I know, and I know what I need.

I also know that my kids benefit when I take my meds. If I don't take them, I keep myself stuck, and I live in a non-coping way, and I want to hide from the world. Will there come a time when I don't need antidepressants anymore? I don't know, but for now I do. I have a family to care for, and they have suffered enough with circumstances beyond their control. It is no time to experiment with an amateur's theory that will probably land me in a more depressed state.

Then there are those people I know who could benefit from antidepressants, but tell me they can't possibly take them as if it is a horrific weakness. When I remind them that I take medications, some have said, "Well, it is okay for you, but I can't." I am not sure what they mean, but what I know is that choosing my battle means taking my meds, regardless of what anyone else thinks, without having to defend my decision to anyone. I don't want to waste time and energy defending what I know I need. So I choose my battles. Going off my meds or defending my need for them is not a battle worth waging.

My lifelong friend bought us tickets to the Women of Faith conference. At first, I didn't want to go because I was sad, and I couldn't get a grip because I had just experienced one of a series of devastating blows. I didn't want to hear a bunch of Christian women telling me I don't have enough faith, because that's what I thought it was all about. (Boy, was I wrong!) But I decided to go mostly for my friend's sake: Joy has such a helper's heart and she was offering me a leg up. I also went because Barbara Johnson, CEO of Spatula Ministries, would be there.

Barbara Johnson wrote a number of books about having struggles in her life, and one of them was finding out her son was gay, at a time when that issue was not discussed. In fact, I bought her book at a library book sale having no idea she was the one who wrote about her gay son. She called her organization Spatula Ministries, because when you found out a person in your family was gay, you had to be scraped off the ceiling with a spatula.

I picked up her book at a garage sale because it was classified as "Humor" on the cover. As I read her story, my brain kept screaming "No, No!" I knew my ex-husband was gay but I didn't want to admit it was real. "Please God," I said, "Don't let this be my life too." Her book forced me to look at my situation and see it for what it was. As the G.I. Joe cartoon says, "Knowing is half the battle." Barbara ended up not coming to the conference. As if her life hadn't already been tough enough with a husband nearly killed in a car wreck, a son who came out of the closet, painful regrets about how she handled the news of the latter, and now she found out she had cancer. But I'm glad I attended anyway.

I cried through most of the conference. It was the singing and the speaking that touched my heart with acceptance. My poor friend Joy, I don't know if she knew what she was getting into by asking me to come, but she silently sat by my side throughout the conference and let it be what it was.

Many well-known Christian women spoke about their everyday challenges, and several even confessed to being on antidepressants and very thankful about it. I couldn't believe it. I had expected a holier-than-thou attitude, and I expected to walk away feeling like even more of a failure than I already was. Two divorces, now antidepressants, working full time while my kids were still young - I thought, "How much lower could I sink? How could I ever share my faith when I messed up my life so badly?"

I have three of the most amazing children I know. We struggled, but those struggles have ultimately been good for us. We are a family that believes in loving others, offering grace, accepting others as they are, and showing compassion. My marriage didn't fail at all from the perspective of my children. Their lives were meant to be, and my world is a better place because of them. All the pain of rejection has melted into nothing because my children are worth infinitely more than me getting my way.

"I want to see myself as God truly sees me..."

So where should I put my energy? What battle will I join and what will I let fly by? I choose to put my energy into family, work, then some fun - gardening, another hobby - something that refreshes me. I want to see myself as God truly sees me; I will put zero effort into becoming what condemning people think I should be.

I was offered a job in special education at my kids' school. I knew I could do really well in that department. I knew I would love the children, but I knew if I did it every day, by the time I got home I'd be spent and impatient with my own kids. So I turned down the job. What decisions do you have to make? What battles are worth taking on? Be prepared to be misunderstood. Say no anyway. Know what you know about yourself and your family. Choose accordingly.

Other disorders in our family include ADD and OCD. ADD is Attention Deficit Disorder, but my friend, Precious, and I like to call it Artists Daring to Dream. My son had OCD (Obsessive Compulsive Disorder) and was struggling in school. His strand of OCD was perfectionism. He would erase his paper until the paper ripped under the friction. He couldn't turn in a paper he didn't think was perfect, so he gave up on turning in homework. He was failing and no one seemed to understand why.

The school counselor, Leigha, took him on. She understood him and worked with him, helping him find ways to cope. She gave him a place to come and sit when things were too overwhelming. As his time in high school drew to a close, I worried that he wouldn't graduate, and I wasn't sure he cared much about it.

I needed to let go, but I started reacting out of fear of what would happen if he didn't graduate. What kind of parent would that make me? I got lost in all the "what if's" even though we were getting help, going to counseling, and working hard on our options." I let him take ownership of the question, "Will he graduate?" And stopped trying to force the issue. When it became less important to me, it seemed to become more important to him. I also give his girlfriend a lot of credit for him graduating. She had a way with him that was so kind and loving, whereas I would get frustrated and cranky.

I'm anything but a perfectionist, and I didn't understand his OCD. Medication and behavior modification all helped, but I still had to give his schooling back to him. I gave him the options of home-schooling, obtaining his GED certificate, or finding some other way to make it through high school, and then I just let go. Wow, he *did* graduate from high school and then went on to graduate from trade school with top honors as a mechanic. I have no regrets for having chosen my battle and not making a new career out of getting him through high school. That was his battle.

I have another son with Attention Deficit and Hyperactivity Disorder (ADHD) who has taught me so much about life. If you know anything about ADHD, you're aware there are amazing things that go with it. One seems to be always sticking up for the underdog. This got him in trouble more times than not because he felt a teacher was being unfair to another student, and he would vocalize it. In fact, when I worked for The Big Brother/Big Sister Organization, my office in the high school building was near the principal's office and the "detention" room. My son would often walk by and give me a salute and take his seat in the detention room, because he had been kicked out of class.

On one of these occasions, I could hear him in the room tapping and making drum noises - kids with ADHD don't sit still very well. It's difficult for them to sit at all. So I peeked in and saw he was drumming away on every possible object in the room, and the vice-principal was in the next office was hearing it all. When I shot Mr. Patton a look halfway between embarrassment and bewilderment, he just smiled knowingly and said, "Oh, he's not hurting anyone and really, I would be more concerned if he was quiet." How grateful I was to the vice-principal, who knew a thing or two about ADHD.

I have heard all the conversations about ADHD. I have heard folks say that kids are over-diagnosed, and they're all just taking pills to keep them quiet. Perhaps you have heard this said, or even think it. My son takes the "pills," but he made the choice to take meds only when he was ready. He was ready when he realized he couldn't pay attention or finish anything like other people. The medications have helped remarkably. It's not about quiet or control; it's about normal functioning. ADD is very real, and we're all very grateful for those pills.

These disorders have affected my children's schooling, and taken up much of my limited energy. I was forced to make decisions to let other things go - important things - but I chose what was best for my children. I was often told that I was making excuses for them, but when my children were diagnosed, they agreed and could see how their disorder was affecting their lives and our lives together. All I could do was love and support them no matter what.

In this case, I looked to the Family Resource Center for help, counseling, and support. This is where I discovered the Readiness to Learn Program (RTL) that supports children who want to stay in school. It was such a relief that the people I worked with at RTL believed me. It was incredible and gave me the energy to do right by my kids.

"Cleaning your house while your kids are still growing is like shoveling the snow before it stops snowing."
--Phyllis Diller, Phyllis Diller's Housekeeping Hints 1966

Now I have to confess; I am a "messy." I prefer explaining it by saying that my kids come first, so there is no time for organizing. Housework has always been a struggle for me. So imagine a messy with a child who is a minimalist and perfectionist with OCD. Imagine a messy with a child who is bouncing off the walls with enough energy for ten people.

Not only that, but my two boys had disorders that were at opposite ends of the spectrum. They loved each other and they hated each other at the same time. Each could not tolerate the other one's disorder. At times, this felt unbearable.

There were a few months when the older one lived somewhere else because he didn't feel safe around his brother's impulsiveness. I had to make a choice to let it be what it was and trust my kids to know what they needed. But I hated it. It broke my heart that we couldn't live together like a normal family, but I was grateful for the couple that took my son in and loved him. They gave him a safe place to be while we all worked through the struggles.

"I went to a support group called Messies Anonymous."

I went to a support group called Messies Anonymous. I'm not kidding; it helped. They gave me permission to let go and not to be so hard on myself. I envy those who have a natural gift for organizing and keeping things picked up. They're always ready for guests. For some of us, it's more difficult. And if you add depression, shame about divorce, shame about a messy house, and children with disorders on opposite ends of the spectrum into the mix, it becomes even more difficult. The last variable is that I am dealing with all this by myself as a single mom. No tag team parenting, just me, all the time, twenty-four/seven.

So I had to choose what I could take on and what I had to let go. I couldn't be the provider for the family, arbiter of conflicts, chief family financial officer, family taxi driver, and Suzy Homemaker all at the same time. I couldn't do it all, and neither can you. Choose what is important, give yourself permission to do what you can, and let the rest go.

How do you get the things done that you have to let go, but that still have to get done? One answer: barter! I had a friend who loves, loves, loves to organize. She helped with my house, and I helped with her garden. I know what you're thinking, but gardening is like therapy for me. To get my hands in dirt is heavenly.

See, I just had to be creative and also give myself permission to get help with what had to be done, but what I really stink at doing. If you have plenty of money you can hire a maid, but if you're pinching pennies, you have to be creative. Trading services is a way to keep you doing what comes naturally while helping you address the dreaded tasks.

I have amazing friends - friends whose kids have disorders too. Some are unsolvable. Like my kids, their kids take responsibility for their OCD and ADHD too. They work with their doctors and learn how to cope. They need to write *their* stories someday! These are some of my wonderful friends who drank coffee and ate chocolate chip cookies with me at the table piled high with school work, bills, and groceries--and maybe even a cat.

To the friends who visited with me in my raspberry patch, who found an empty place in the midst of laundry on the couch to sit and visit, who saw *me* and not my mess; thank you from the bottom of my heart. Thank you, friends who pitched in for big events like graduations and parties, and who helped us move in and move out of houses. You are my heroes.

Maybe your children have disorders. Maybe you have a child with Fetal Alcohol Syndrome (FAS) or affect. Many adopted children have this disorder. Maybe their disorder has forever changed your life. I have friends who have adopted children with FAS. The children look fine and are high functioning, but their brains are truly damaged, and there's a disconnection at some level. I have watched these friends in the trenches; I've seen their heartache at being misunderstood. I've sat with them as they've wept, wondering what they've done wrong. I've seen these parents being accused of being the problem by well-meaning friends, or even counselors. Yet I have been inspired by their strength.

Fetal Alcohol children can't be fixed, and when they become adults, they are completely on their own. They may even see themselves as normal and rational. Their decisions and choices seem perfectly right to them. So you can't help or advise them. In fact, they think everyone else is the problem. They are charming and sweet, and yet have this disconnect that makes life difficult for them and their families.

See, some disorders have pills or therapies that the folks who have them can take and function at a fairly normal level. But how do you cope with a condition for which there is no cure, no pill, no therapy? How do you live with an unresolvable story?

A woman speaking at a luncheon talked about adopting children and all the blessings and wonderful stories. I was so touched, but felt even sadder for my friends whose adoption experience had been so difficult with their FAS child. Afterward, I shook the speaker's hand and thanked her.

I told her about my friends and their FAS child and how they loved him so much, but that their adoption experience had become such a struggle. This speaker started to cry. She told me the rest of her own story: How hard it has been with her own adopted children and their own disorders. I would have much rather heard that story.

"How do you live with an unresolvable story?"

We often don't want to tell unresolved stories because other people don't know what to do with them. Many people don't know what to do with something that can't be fixed. They tend to fix, blame, judge, and minimize. First the fixing mechanism kicks in with unsolicited advice, then the blame game because someone must be responsible for the imperfection, then "shoulds" with all their pontificating judgment, and finally minimizing, accusing people of looking for excuses for what is their own "irresponsibility."

People can't help it; they don't like an unresolved story. In fact, they don't really take people's stories into account at all, since they are essentially all unfinished stories that may or may not result in a happy ending.

Well, we weren't created for hopelessness; we were created for hope. My friends have learned to choose their battles and modeled their courage to me. It wasn't easy, but they learned to laugh, and I am so honored to laugh with them.

Just Wondering:

Have you looked at your life and thought, "How did this happen?"

How do we choose what is next? How do we live in the midst of life? Disorders, divorce, death?

Are you choosing your battles or trying to do it all?

What can you let go of?

What is a priority?

What changes would you like to make?

What is one small step that will help you be true to your self and your values while letting go of things?

What would permission look like?

Write yourself a permission slip to "let go of_____."

Choose your battles and choose to remember your dream.

Even if your passion is on hold, on the shelf or in the trunk, it is still yours. You still have a purpose right now it may look a little different than you anticipated. By choosing your battles, you clear the path a little for yourself and your needs. When you start letting go of doing and being everything and embracing that you are enough, when you take time to breath and nap, you will find the energy to go on. The adventure is your story, your journey.

Be in it!

Choose it; choose your battles!

Choose life and adventure and good things will happen.

As Fran Fisher of the Academy of Coach Training (ACT) used to say,

"Are you dancing in the moment?"

Give yourself permission.

Choose your battles.

11

No Shoulding. Being the Victim of Well Intenders.

"Just say no to should, need to, and must."
--Laurie Hardie

Choosing our battles gives us respite from feeling we are somehow responsible for everything in life. Learning to let go of those things that aren't most important includes letting go of some of the mean things people say. If these things come from our friends, we know they mean well, but lack some basic relational skills.

I don't understand why people think it is their job to comment on things that aren't any of their business. But when they do, I wish they could be smart, or compassionate, or at least original while they're at it. It's one of my pet peeves. My guess is that they somehow feel threatened like what is happening to me could happen to them, and they get scared.

Here are some throw-away phrases people use when they are engaging in this pet peeve:

"It was meant to be."

"Everything happens for a reason."

"It's for the best."

"Well at least you still have __________ ."

(Another leg? Another eye?)

"Have you prayed about this?"

Have you felt the sting of these phrases? Now, let me let everyone off the hook by saying I've *said* all of those things, too. I have been one of "those" people with all the answers. I know I just had to have a trite saying in order to protect myself. After all, if something bad could happen to someone for no apparent reason, then it could happen to me, too. So these words and phrases sort of became my defense to ward off evil, if you will.

Truth be told, I didn't think about what I was really saying very much until I became the unwilling recipient of some of my own pat answers. It wasn't fun to be on the receiving end of those phrases.

The first time I had my own words thrown back at me was when I had a miscarriage. I was devastated. I had picked out names, made plans; I so wanted the baby, and I lost it at four months. I needed to grieve, but apparently other people would have been more comforted by providing the magic words to end my grieving. Or was it to console themselves, because they really had no answer as to why it had happened?

They said things that made God out to be some sort of impulsive cosmic killjoy, a masochistic meanie: "God wanted that baby more than you did." Someone else told me, "Laurie, it was meant to be." I wanted to tell this Job's Comforter that it sure fooled me because I thought it *wasn't* meant to, but how shocked I now am because it was meant to be after all! Such throw-away phrases must comfort the speaker, but it didn't do much for me.

In a similar vein I was told, "Everything happens for a reason." It should be illegal to say such a thing unless someone *knows* the reason. Only God knows that, and He isn't telling. Some times I wish He would explain so people who think they speak on his behalf would quit putting Him in such a bad light.

The thing is, most of these types of inconsiderate comments are really about the person saying them, not about the person who is hurting. When I was hurting, I couldn't see that. So I just got angry and defensive and thought I must really be a loser for all God's goodness to be heaped on me with such pain. Eventually I laughed at people's absurd explanations, but in the moment, they can still really sting.

The church announcements in the bulletin asked us to pray for a woman's family because she had a miscarriage. All of us in the church knew how long and hard they had been trying for a baby, and I felt so sad for her. Back then, our church had a "meet and greet" break, so that Sunday I sought her out and said, "I know this must be so hard for you." She said, "Yes, but it's meant to be." Her comment felt more like resignation than theological confidence in God's wisdom, so I said, "Really?" Surprised, she looked at me as if speechless.

I told her that when I had a miscarriage people said the most thoughtless, hurtful things to me and that I didn't claim to know why it happened, but that didn't make it any less devastating. It was tragic and that was all there was to it. Her eyes filled with tears and her husband was behind her nodding. That's what hurting people want to hear. It's a tragedy, and it does not bring comfort when folks speculate about why it happened.

In fairness to the misguided comforters, they don't really know what to say, so they go with the first thing that comes to mind, or maybe even repeat something they heard before.

What do these throwaway comments say about God? Real comforters are not supposed to be privy to God's sovereign purposes. For us mere mortals, because we feel the helplessness of not knowing why, we are able to deeply feel another's pain. I guess it's enough for me to acknowledge someone else's pain while it's God's work to manage the universe wisely. I don't try to do His job or make silly guesses about His motives.

When a dear friend of mine died, I called his wife, who was also a close friend, right away. I had not the slightest idea what to say. All I could eke out was a feeble, "I heard." She told me he died instantly, and I almost commented on the blessing of dying that way, but restrained myself. Sudden death was certainly no comfort to her. Here was the intolerable deal: He's gone and she is alone. She now has to deal with all his stuff and be strong for her kids. I wanted to say something cleverly comforting, but all I could do was tell her that I loved her.

I can be as thoughtless as the next person, but I am using suffering in the lives of others as a cue to be more thoughtful about what it is like for them, more than what it is like for me. That usually means being quick to listen and slow to speak. It's more important just to be there, to be available.

I used to want to fix everyone by offering advice: "Have you tried this? I think you should____." Boy, what was I thinking? What I have discovered is people are actually really smart, and if they are having problems or they are sad, they probably just need some affirming (if bewildered) person to listen. They usually have already thought through every scenario. Hey, if they want to know what I think, they can ask me. But if truth be told, I'm as clueless about the why as they are.

I realized that when I found out someone was in a really bad situation, I would get scared for *myself* and try to "help" *them*. I had to hear from a counselor that my helpfulness was really my attempt to explain away my own doubts. It was essentially no help at all to other people.

Also, my counselor modeled to me who I could be when others turned to me for help. I trusted her because I knew she had been through suffering, and she didn't react out of fear to my problems. Instead, she listened and shared stories, assuring me I was not the only person to experience these kinds of things. She told me about other people who had been through similar situations and that helped me tremendously.

When I was still raising my kids, I decided that my daughter could keep her horse after the divorce. The challenge was that horses are expensive to care for, but I found a place to keep her for free. I worked extra jobs to pay for grain, hay, and horseshoes. I knew that my twelve-year-old daughter would be devastated if she lost her horse. Every book on divorce that I read at the time said that divorce is the hardest on kids who are 12.

But advice-givers told me I was foolish to not sell the horse—some even chided me for not getting rid of our beloved family dog! I was determined that though divorce meant their parents were broken up, it didn't mean they had to lose everything in the world that brought joy or comfort. I knew that the animals in our life were a healing balm for my children's souls, so I kept

Katie the horse and Bear the dog. Some people were so convinced I was being irresponsible by keeping the animals that they refused to help me at all. Well done, ye enforcers of responsibility! Years have gone by, but I have never once regretted keeping those animals for my children.

Some well-intentioned folks ask things like, "Have you prayed about it?" Probably because things didn't seem to be turning out well. Little did they know I do little else except pray when I feel helpless. Still, I actually had a pastor's wife tell me that I wouldn't have had such a difficult life, if I had prayed more before I married my husband. Nice lady, but such bad theology.

The gospel is about God doing for us what we could not do for ourselves. The God of the New Testament doesn't punish us for not praying enough, but He must be sad because some of us think we can manipulate Him into doing what we want by using pious acts. Sorry, but the true God of the universe can't be controlled by our whims.

"That's underestimating God,

the only one who has it all figured out."

According to a theologian named C. S. Lewis, prayer is about our own transformations, not about manipulating God. Look, we live in a fallen world where life happens and things happen in a broken way. What we do with what happens is not about figuring it all out, because when you think you have figured it out, you're wrong anyway. That's underestimating God, the only one who has it all figured out.

I spent way too much time trying to figure out my missteps and beating myself up for how I could have been so deceived. It hasn't done me any good, and it doesn't do the equally deceived Job's (Job from the Bible) Comforters any good either. So I invite you to journey with me in the adventure of resolving not to beat yourself up. If we look at the path ahead, we can know there are benches and gardens and resting places, because that is more in keeping with God's character. Second guessing yourself doesn't solve the problem, and it doesn't matter if you prayed hard enough - God is not impressed. It is what it is, and you are where you are, and it is the best place to be for your next step.

"We get to find our parts in it and we keep movin', like a dance in the moment rather than a death march."

You are acknowledging the reality of your seemingly impossible situation, and that is the stuff with which God will do something. Life happens, and we get to be in it. We don't have to waste time trying to undo it (as if we could!) We get to learn, grow, and move forward zigging and zagging. We get to find our parts in it and we keep movin', like a dance in the moment rather than a death march.

Best-selling author, Dr. Larry Crabb, talks about a foundational faith showing what we really believe about God. Many well-intentioned people don't show a true foundation of faith, because the things they say to hurt people don't reflect a desperate need for God's grace, but rather highlight a false belief that they are doing fine; that it is the walking wounded who have a lot to learn. I guess the gift in being the walking wounded is that I harbor no illusion that I have anything that can obligate God to push my agenda. Funny, my agenda in writing a book like this was to get self-righteous people to admit their error, but self-righteous people don't read books like this in the first place. And on the off chance that they do, they don't see themselves as the ones in need of changing.

I'm grateful for my pain, because it has made me a better friend. It has kept me from assuming others are in trouble because they made a mistake. I have learned that really bad things can happen to really good people. It's just life in a fallen world. I used to threaten God and say, "If I'm going through this just so I can help others, I'm going to be really ticked."

The truth is, whatever we go through is what we get to go through. So something bad happened, so what? What will we do with it? We can get angry and take it out on others, but it isn't about them and it often isn't about us either. It may be about living in a world where things happen for reasons we don't know. We live in a world where people get sick, and people die, and some people have perfect kids who don't require much effort, and some work their tails off for rebellious children.

So, here is what I can do. I can take the following words and phrases out of my vocabulary: should, you should, you need to, and you must. Who am I to say what someone else needs to do? Of course there are exceptions, but for the most part, I believe I can be a better friend when I listen more, tell less, and ask good questions that are validating rather than condemning. Why? Because it is a better formula that works? No, because it reflects the truth of living in a world that is broken, where sometimes things go awry and sometimes things go my way.

And for the blessings, I can take very little credit. I can thoroughly enjoy the good stuff and for goodness sake, of course, I can conclude that the bad stuff really stinks, because it does. Here is where hope comes in: There is someone who will someday take all the stinky stuff and make sense of it so that the walking wounded will be the big winners when all they could do was trust.

"...avoiding the urge to flee, to fix, and to farm out."

I talked about avoiding the urge to flee, to fix, and to farm out. I guess another is avoiding the urge to "placate" by saying something trite. Think about what you can learn by not adding a trite saying that does not reflect reality. Once when a child at school was killed in a car crash, a teen said to the student's parents, "It's like Billy Joel said, 'Only the good die young.'" Hewas parroting what sounds right because he didn't know any better, but grown-ups sometimes still say trite things when others are hurting.

Makc your fcar part of thc advcnturc, and stand by thc hurting and say nothing, just give a hug or a nod. When you're in a situation where someone is dealing with a very difficult thing, think about what the other person needs. What would you want if you were in the same situation? Before I realized what it was that bothered me, I just got mad and defensive. Now, I actually recognize it and acknowledge it, and I am learning to have some fun with it.

A pet peeve that really gets me going is when people tell me what I "should" do. My friends and I call it "shoulding on me." "You know what you should do?" Most of the time it is innocent, using *should, need to,* and *must.* It's like fingernails on the chalkboard to me. In fact, when my clients tell me what they should do, need to do, have to do, or must do, I challenge them about what they "ought" to do.

When we should, must, need, or have to do something, our choices are taken away. What circumstance is forcing your hand? Do you want to do it? I feel some defenses going up right now. We "have" to serve, we "must" do our part, we "should" help out. Really it isn't the words; it's the attitude.

Take charitable giving. Some people say I must give more, but it's not how much, but *how* one gives: *God loves a cheerful giver.* (2 Corinthians 9:7) If you were in a difficult situation and you "needed" something from someone, would you want it from someone who "should, must, needed to, or had to" (but didn't necessarily want) to do it for you? Neither does God. He wants people to do things for others that come from the heart, not from having to.

When you want to, you do it cheerfully; when you have to, resentment builds. When I am meeting with someone and I hear them say, "I should" do something or "I must" go somewhere, then I ask them, "Do you want to?" If the answer is a resounding yes, then I ask them to own it by saying, "I want to go." If something doesn't go the way you planned or hoped, you can take responsibility for it. After all, you weren't forced to go; you chose to go.

Of course, by now we know that if things don't go as we planned, it's okay because this life is an adventure, after all.

Should

Must

Need to

Have to

When I began realizing the power and destruction of the above words, I tried to be more aware of when I used them. I would catch myself saying one of these words and think, "Should I do it? Do I want to do it?" Even simple things like, "I should get the dishes done." Should I? Or do I want to? In reality, I *do* want to. I want my kitchen to be clean; it benefits me and it becomes a choice for better things in my life rather than a duty. I become the chooser, not the victim. You could even go as far as to ask, "What's in it for me?" If the answer is, "A clean house," then I'm on board!

Start Recognizing When You Are "Shoulding"

The next consideration is, are you "shoulding" on your children, friends, or family? If you are, what words can you use instead? I'm an encourager, so when someone tells me something she wants to do, I tell her she should do that. In my admittedly self-protective effort to not be the one to blame when things go awry, I started asking questions rather than making statements, and so I would ask, "What would it take for you to make that happen?"

If I saw it was something they really wanted to do or try, then I changed my "should" to a dare. A "double-dog" dare, if necessary. The words of "should, must, need to, want to" have a negative bent to them; no wonder they're such downers. I want life-giving words like, "I want to____." It doesn't mean we never do anything we don't want to do. It doesn't mean we become selfish and don't do anything we think we "should" do. It means we reframe the situation and think about it differently. We take responsibility for what we say and what we do because ultimately *no one can make anyone else do anything they don't want to do.* We have no one else to blame for our choices, even if it sometimes *feels* like we have no choice.

How often have we heard others gossiping—sharing their frustrations about others—and they say something like, "If she would just do thus and so, things would be fine." We've all heard something like that, said something like that, or been the victim of such words. We feel helpless when someone is struggling, so we come up with a practical solution, something we are just sure could work. We want to get that person with the problem just to be okay. Maybe the advice we wish they would take is something that worked for us, so of course it will work for everyone else. Wanting someone to just do something so we won't have to worry any more is about us, not them.

"We want to get that person with the problem just to be okay."

When you find yourself "*shoulding*" others, ask yourself, "Who is this about?" By offering "shoulds", "need tos," "musts" and "have tos," are you robbing them of an adventure? A life experience? What if I told every woman whose husband came out of the closet to do what I did? I would certainly not want to take responsibility for the disaster that could possibly follow.

"Resisting the urge to offer platitudes and advice is a zillion times harder than offering "shoulds.""

No, what I want to do is listen, hear, and love well. I don't want to be about telling others what to do. I want to be about supporting the adventure, no matter how nervous it makes me. I want to be in it for the long haul with others, so I will hold my tongue. Resisting the urge to offer platitudes and advice is a zillion times harder than offering "shoulds."

We are not here to fix others; we are here to love and be loved. We are here to hold the hands of the suffering, not "should" them and shame because life didn't turn out how they hoped. "Shoulding" people is essentially blaming them for their predicament. And really what does it matter? If someone is in a situation, all the blaming in the world isn't going to change it.

What's important is how the adventure continues and who the supporting performers are. I wouldn't be where I am today if it weren't for all my amazing supporting cast: People who loved me well and fought the urge to blame me and should on me. I want to be like them, I don't want to put blame on the ones I love, and I don't want to should on them. I want to live the adventure. How about you?

No more shoulds?

On you or anyone else.

I dare you.

I double dog dare you.

Another pet peeve is gossip. Yes I do it, but I am working really hard at recognizing and acknowledging my part in it. How come I join in? What is so enticing about gossip? In the meantime, while I'm trying to be better about it, I'm practicing:

Good gossip

I have a strategy that helps me when I want to "should" on others. It's good gossip, and it's so much better in the long run. Gossip is destructive, even if it sometimes has a kernel of truth, because the motive behind it is usually somehow about feeling powerful by having "critical information." Sometimes it feels good to have a laugh at the expense of someone else. If we talk about others, it keeps the focus off of our own faults.

Rise Above It

The first step is to recognize that you are gossiping. You don't have to be a psychiatrist to know what you're up to. When you recognize it, ask yourself what you got out of it: power, fun, revenge, attention? As a result of this self-examination, I'm sorry to say that I love gossip. I love that it brings camaraderie: all of us united in hurting and laughing at another person, each of us motivated by our own pain.

So now what I *want* to do when someone starts to gossip about someone, if I am not gutsy enough to stop it or say I don't want to participate, is walk away. I excuse myself - so maybe I wasn't brave - but I take myself out of the equation. And believe me, it isn't easy. Walking away gives the impression I'm not interested, and I am. I also risk being perceived as self-righteous, which I hope I'm not.

It seems fun, unless the gossip is about someone I care about, then it hurts me too. Will I stick up for my friend, while others are having a good time at their expense? We radio people are entertainers. We love to make people laugh, so when we get a good subject—look out. If I have my wits about me, I like to come back at gossip with something good about that person, and that's what "good gossip" is.

I want to say something like, "What I know about Jane Doe is ________." And then I want to say something truthful like: She has a big heart, she is kind, or she helped me out with a tough situation—something true. See, I *want* to be about integrity and gossip destroys integrity, mine particularly. And, oh yeah, it also contributes to a profound sense of insecurity because I can't help but think that, if they can talk about Jane behind her back, they will certainly talk about me after I leave the room.

Good Gossip Is Life Giving

Ending gossip is kind of like going on a diet. If we try to quit cold turkey, we cut ourselves off and we become isolated and left out. It can become too much to bear, and we allow ourselves just one little tidbit. Of course, if we couch what we say in a prayer request or say it with a wrinkled brow that shows how genuinely concerned we claim to be, then we can justify it as not really being gossip. It's like chocolate. It's so good, how can it be hurtful (and haven't scientists shown how healthy chocolate really is?)

So really it isn't about stopping the outward behavior, it is about a change of heart that causes us to embrace the Golden Rule: I won't do to others what I would hate for them to do to me. And if it hurts me, it hurts you and everyone else. I don't want to be about hurting people; I want to be the kind of person who is a blessing to others.

So let's get real and internalize what we are supposed to hate about gossip:

What do you love about it? An Exercise

(Write this down and you can tear it up or burn your true confessions.)

What I love about gossip is_____.

Being the first to break a story?

Telling others something bad about someone else?

The intrigue of it all?

How everyone unites to add to the story?

It makes me feel powerful?

It is sweet revenge?

Keep going. Come on, fess up.

What is it about gossip that is so enticing and addicting?

What can you do to start changing your behavior around gossip?

What has worked for you in the past?

Some people walk away; some speakout; some exchange good gossip for bad.

What will your tactic be?

Let's Change All Gossip To Good Gossip.

Why do we want to hurt someone else, because it makes us feel better somehow? Evaluate the information you're sharing with others. So what if they don't get the dirt from us first? What if we know something but we don't share it?

Where does integrity fit into this? The challenge is to want to work on practicing good gossip. Offer a good report about people to their peers. Share good things.

Spread good gossip. In order to get started, it requires looking for the good in others:

What is something good about each person you work with?

How about the people you live with?

What I love about (insert name here) is ___________.

Pet peeves, pat answers, and gossip wreak havoc in the world. Be aware, pay attention, and think about what you would like others to say to you and about you. Others speak kindly about you, so return the favor.

"Pet peeves, pat answers, and gossip wreak havoc in the world."

Just Wondering:

What are your Pet Peeves?

What ridiculous things do people say or do that drive you nuts?

Can you make a comedy routine about it?

Draw a picture?

Have you been "shoulded" on lately?

How did it feel?

What would you have rather heard?

Have you "shoulded" on anyone lately?

Can you apologize and say what you really meant to say?

Or, did you really mean it and you want to fix?

Then don't go back to the person you "should-ed" on, take some time to look at what it is that's causing you to want to "make" another person do something.

What is it stirring in you? Fear? Uncertainty? That's about you.

Want to work on it?

Find a safe friend to talk it over with. You can also hire a life coach, counselor, or spiritual director. This is your adventure, and it will bring you to a place of love and acceptance.

Have you been the victim of well in-tenders?

Have you been the one offering the "well intended" pat answers?

Think about how you would have liked to have been treated.

What will you do different next time you are in the situation?

What do you think about "should?"

What are your pet peeves?

Is there something deeper about them, than just being irritating?

What is it that really bothers you about it?

DID NOT SEE THAT COMING

Some peeves are just that--things that drive you nuts. But some have a deeper value, and looking at them may uncover a treasure.

12

Having Enough Gratitude, Grace, And Giving

"He is richest who is content with the least, for content is the wealth of nature."
--Socrates

"In all things give thanks."
--Ephesians 5:20

Dealing with the pat answers of others can be draining and hurtful. In fact, pat answers just make it easier to get caught up in what we don't have and how life may not be working so great for us. Taking control by thinking about how we will respond in such instances gives us back a little bit of ourselves. We can make a difference with how we respond to others.

"I will breathe, and this is just another adventure."

So many times I have felt as though I am drowning, and I am never going to get that needed breath of air. I'm not talking just treading water; I'm drowning. If I give any attention to that feeling, it can take me under. But as soon as I recognize hopelessness, I force myself to remember that I will make it. I will breathe, and this is just another adventure.

One time, I was really struggling, and I didn't want to force myself to remember. I didn't want to let go of my despair. I called my cousin Donna and she said, "I don't let myself go there." That was all I needed to hear. Donna, ten years my junior, reminded me that there is power in positive thinking, not false, but positive truth. She didn't assure me that, "Everything is going to be fine," but rather "You are going to make it" and this will not kill me.

There's a verse in the Message version of the New Testament that says, "Don't fret or worry. Instead of worrying, pray. Let petitions and praises shape your worries into prayers, letting God know your concerns." A few verses later, the author, Paul, says, "Summing it all up friends, I'd say you'll do best by filling your minds and meditating on things true, noble, reputable, authentic, compelling, gracious – the best, not the worst; the beautiful, not the ugly; things to praise, not things to curse." Paul continues, "Do that and God, who makes everything work together, will work you into His most excellent harmonies."

I'm not one to minimize feelings. I do tend to disregard my instincts, and when it comes to fear, I can easily start to lose ground. I lay in bed at night and worry about:

How am I going to raise these kids?

How am I going to love them enough?

Give them what they need?

Be there for them?

How can I keep being the one to wipe their tears and field their frustrations? This fear leads to "not enough" thinking.

God's not enough. I'm not enough. I don't have enough. I don't do enough. I tread water in the ocean of I'm Not Enough and I get sucked in. The facts are there. Not enough money to pay all the bills or get the things we "want." I guess my basic needs are being met, but not to the level of my dreams. Yet we are surviving. Still, how many different ways can I serve ramen noodles and refried beans? Then I remember the verse in Philippians: "Don't fret or worry. Instead of worrying, pray. Let petitions and praises shape your worries into prayers, letting God know your concerns."

I am enough.

When Donna reminded me not to go to thoughts of resignation, it reminded me of something I used to do when my kids were little. I would start each day writing in my journal, and I would write down five things I was grateful for. I let that habit slip by the wayside when things got bad.

So I started over, beginning each day by finding five things I was grateful for. At first it was hard, because, as I thought, what can a drowning person be grateful for? It wasn't long before I could come up with ten or more things easily every day. Did it fix my situation? As my friend Jenn often says, "Hell to the no!" But it changed my thoughts and my focus. I could look for what was good and let what we had be enough.

I suddenly was not wasting so much of my brainpower on the negative what if's and fears. I have learned about faith and the power of believing: believing I am going to make it, believing that this is enough. Believing and gratitude sustained me. Gratitude and believing were my life raft. When I was growing up in a small town, on a small island, no church building was nearby. Some people who lived by us, but attended church in another town, held a Sunday school at the community clubhouse. Some neighbors with a station wagon would pick up me and my sister, along with other kids around the lagoon, and take us to Sunday school, where we sang hymns and fun kids songs. I especially liked the song "Count Your Blessings" because it sounded good in harmony.

Count your blessings,

Name them one by one.

Count your blessings; see what God has done.

It is really easy to focus on and count our griefs, sorrows, and disappointments, but it takes more of an effort to focus on and count our blessings. So I began to rest in "count your blessings," though compared to others who seemed to have a novel full of blessings, I thought I only had a haiku.

It felt like not enough, and I often found myself comparing my situation to others, which was followed by a downward spiral. Then I would remember to look for what I could honestly be grateful for. Sometimes that meant looking back.

Trying to get sympathy when I felt like I didn't have enough, almost always backfired. I got a jolt when people would remind me of what I already knew was the case. They would remind me of what I already had, and enumerate individual blessings like having a roof over my head, having enough to eat, and having loved ones. Of course, their intentions were good and they were right – but still, those were reminders not to complain, just suck it in and buck up.

I did have things to be grateful for, but what I really hated was being told I wasn't grateful enough. I should have been grateful that I was grateful. Eventually, I was able to look at all the good things about my life with gratitude. I have also noticed that another shift always happens in me when I can find things to be grateful for. I then seem to become more creative and resourceful.

The day came when all three of my children were nearly raised. The empty nest was approaching, and my youngest son chose to live with his dad. Even with a full time job, I couldn't keep an empty house, and it seemed I had no other choice than to move in with my sister and her husband. They took me in with open arms.

They loved me and looked out for me, and I never wanted to leave. I stayed with them for two years. My bed faced an armoire with an object on top - big black wooden letters all in caps that spell "BELIEVE," a birthday present from my friend, Wendy. I put that word there as a reminder to never give up. I love the word "believe" because I believe it saved my life. I have a purpose and living it out means believing the purpose can come to pass, even when it seems impossible. I believe that if people believe they will find their paths no matter what, even when life gets in the way.

Parenting had been such a huge part of my life, but now with the two older kids on their own, and the youngest with his dad, I didn't know what to do when it abruptly came to a halt. I had begun taking steps toward the next era of my life so

I had a plan, but I would look up at those beautiful black letters, and all I could see were the center three letters, "-lie-." Lie!

Be -lie- ve

It's all a lie.

"To say you believe is nothing more than pretending it's all good when it's not!" Those negative words haunted me; they taunted me. Everything I was and hoped to be was wrapped up in believing and maybe it was all a big fat lie. I felt the rug had been pulled out from under me. I couldn't process this. It kept me awake many a night.

"Again, serendipity came into play..."

Then I felt the challenge to write a book revive in me. I knew I wanted to offer hope to other single parents, and to believe the lie and give up in defeat would be just what the enemy wanted. Again, serendipity came into play and I met my publishing coach, Patrick, and within months the book was well under way.

When I looked up at the word "believe" one night, I noticed what I saw was EVE. I was on the eve of my "what's next." It all seemed to make sense, a few nights later I only noticed BE. Just be. And now I see the whole word again.

BELIEVE

In coaching, I have seen my clients begin to voice their dreams and doors fly open. I don't know if it is some serendipitous magic or if the doors, invisible, were always ajar. All I know is when I start believing and take the steps, things begin to happen. Our brains need a break from the disaster, disappointments, and frustrations of trying to raise kids alone, or from the common worries of everyday life, or from the gnawing feelings that it isn't enough. You have enough. Let your eyes be open to the possibilities.

Wonder

Dream

Believe

So back to the question, "What do I want?" After the kids were all graduated and I was on with my life, in the midst of living my dream, I couldn't figure out why I didn't feel "happy." Things were going well. I had finished raising the kids. I was working a job I really loved and hosting a radio show with my coaching partner. What was wrong with me? I realized I needed time to grieve and let go of what my life had been.

Sometimes prisoners can't function in the world when they're released. The freedom and the need to make choices are unsettling, and there is a pull to go back to what is familiar. It is important to give ourselves permission to move on, to do things for ourselves. I don't have anyone to answer to, pick up, drop off, problem-solve with, or be at their beck and call. Now, I am truly single. It takes some getting used to.

Again, there was a choice in this. I can choose to be happy, to embrace my freedom, and to let go of nagging guilt that some how I am neglecting someone by doing what I want when I want. I have the opportunity to change some of the tapes in my head and get some new messages. It seems to go back to the "fake it till you make" it theory. I will say it and then it will begin to be.

The weird thing is that while I was raising my kids, even through the tough times, I felt happy. My life was full and busy, and I had a purpose. I was needed. Then when it was over, I had to take the time to re-evaluate my purpose. I had been taking tiny steps toward my dream. When I was free to do it with more energy and gusto, it surprised me that I wasn't thrilled about it.

We each have the power to tell ourselves what we need to know. We can be the ones to speak truth into our own lives. It takes some realizing and deciding and remembering to do it. It will happen and you can move to the "What's next?" It seems funny: The good things take work. I am choosing to be happy and giving myself permission to enjoy my life. What are you choosing?

"...be the Voice."

I am so grateful that I made the choice to "be the Voice." I am so glad I didn't stay where I was and accept it as, "This is as good as it gets," or fall into feigned gratitude, "Well, at least I have a job." I wanted more. I believed life had more to offer despite the heartache and disappointment and fears I was experiencing.

Looking at those striking black letters that spelled that amazing word while in the midst of startling change, I wavered for a moment and listened to another voice. It suggested that believing is a lie we conjure up to make ourselves feel better. But I remember the truth now, and the truth really will set you free.

To believe is no lie. It is life!

Just Wondering;

Looking back on some unpleasant past experiences, (sorry) what can you see now that you couldn't see then?

What were the gifts disguised by disaster?

What did you learn from those experiences?

What are you grateful for?

What does "false" gratitude mean to you?

How does "should" fit into the mix of being grateful?

What surprises have you discovered in difficult situations?

How might your gratitude look different for you now?

Is there a situation that is difficult or unpleasant that you can begin to see as an adventure, in fact a "gold panning" expedition?

Rather than "hoping" for an end to a tough situation, can you begin to wonder about and believe your "next"?

I have heard so many people say, "I don't dare." Been there, done that—not a good idea. I dare you to try again. Take what you have learned and try again.

It's easy to get lost in "not enough." In fact, living in deficit destroys our souls. If you have to live with not enough, find the places of enough. Look for the adventure of your next steps. Life sometimes seems to steal your dreams and break your heart.

But belief, a strong spirit, and gratitude can open doors you never imagined possible. It is not a guaranteed formula and things may not change overnight, but they may begin taking different shapes and you may begin stepping into areas that will enhance your "What's next?"

Dream

Believe

Choose

I dare you to take just one little step toward your dream.

13

Nurturing the Dream
Remembering how to Breathe

"The future belongs to those who believe in the beauty of their dreams."

--Eleanor Roosevelt

You are enough.

You have enough.

You do enough.

Gratitude took me to a place of believing there was more. Gratitude and thinking about what I love reminded me that the way things are now is not as good as it gets. Once I embraced uncertainty and believed I could be more, the doors flew open. Step-by-step, I walked toward my dream.

It wasn't the way I had planned. It was much slower and a path with more switchbacks than I cared for, but the journey was in motion. I still have down days, disappointments, and times of struggle.

So what is different? I am on the path. My dream and belief keeps me going. I get up wondering about life, rather than being worried that the other shoe is about to drop and that I'm deluded if I think I am ever going to actually make it. Now, even during the toughest times, I can say with full conviction, that this is only a bump in the road, a mere diversion. I'm on my way.

I wonder if you have been thinking about your dream and your passion. Has thinking or writing what you're grateful for or what you love stirred anything? What is or was your dream? What are you passionate about? What is it that you so love doing that you lose track of time while doing it? Once you remember the dream and give yourself permission to entertain your renewed passion, you've made a great start. The trick is to hold on to that renewed dream and passion in the midst of living the life of a single parent, because for you and me, survival and the needs of our kids trump everything else.

"I wonder if you have been thinking about your dream and your passion."

Even though the higher calling of the single parent is the parenting part, it doesn't mean death to a vision for the future. Dreams get put on hold, but they don't have to die. Putting them on the shelf is not the same as putting them in the grave. It's possible to keep them alive. It's possible to add logs to the fire, let their coals cast their slow, steady heat, and enjoy the warmth of the embers. When I say, "add logs to the fire," I mean to take concrete steps toward your dream while you fulfill the parenting role.

I started doing mock radio shows. In some ways, they seemed silly in those days, because I didn't have the technology or means to do a professional show. Nowadays, there is blog radio and podcasting, so it's even more possible to produce a convincing show. Even with my primitive methods, I had fun interviewing friends.

"...take concrete steps toward your dream while you fulfill the parenting role."

A great by-product of my mock broadcasts was the curiosity and growing interest of my friends. I learned new skills, like computer editing, as I created in my spare time and had a blast doing it. It was all amateur, which may seem anticlimactic since I had been in radio. I had been used to having all the equipment I needed. Low tech though it was, it was great fun and amazing to realize I could actually do something this creative.

The first CD I sent out wasn't great, but it was a start. It led to several radio interviews and...voila! I suddenly had REAL audio to work with and to send out. Next, I worked on proposals. I had no idea if I would ever send them out, but it gave me a place to describe my dream of a coaching radio show. See, I was finding ways to keep the dream alive!

What are the tools of your trade?

Can you use them to volunteer?

For example, are you are a musician? Why not do some fun free concerts for the love of your craft?

Whenever I got discouraged I would listen to coaching shows. My good friend and coach, "R," would remind me there is room for all of us and for our dreams.

What is it you love?

What is something you can do to keep what you love alive?

Does volunteering fit in?

How about teaching others what you love?

Do these questions stir up any ideas?

What has occurred to you? Write it down.

Tell a safe friend.

I dare you.

What can you do to nurture the dream and keep it alive, until you have the time and energy to devote yourself fully to it? I found that in making it fun and playful, I was actually laying the groundwork. Every little step makes a difference. Print some business cards and hand them out. There are places online where you can get the cards for free, so you can even experiment with wording and design. Once you hand them out, you're starting to network, making connections. Soon, one or two people will get on board with you.

People love to be part of an energetic movement, and when you love your dream you will be energized, and your passion will draw others. I was resentful of my dream because I couldn't make it happen. It was too big. How dare it be so big! But when I started making little efforts toward it, just for fun, guess what? It began to come together. Once I made an audio tape for a job opening. Well, I didn't get the job—it was a long shot—but applying and making connections was energizing! It got me back into the world I loved.

"No" is a viable option

Sometimes I felt like I was on a treadmill going nowhere fast. Why apply for a job I couldn't get? Here's why: It was about action, being brave, stepping out, and taking a risk. One more "no" put me that much closer to a yes. Believe me, that is an empowering thought. It fills your cup.

Soon I had famous radio people leaving messages on my phone—saying no. Someone I heard on the radio every day was calling me and leaving me a "no" message, but I would respond back and thank him or her for taking the time to call me. "Oh and by the way, Sir, can you give me your professional opinion about how I might improve? I value what you think. What do you think I should work on?"

Ask for help. ASK, ASK, ASK, ASK, ASK! What could happen? He already said no once. Swallow your pride and take a risk.

Risk

Ask

I discovered something revolutionary, and you can discover it too. It's worth about a zillion bucks. It's this: "No" is an acceptable answer. There are only so many No's before you get the Yes. When someone says No, you are closer to the Yes you long for. If you work in sales, you know you have to get like a hundred No's before you get one Yes.

So start counting those No's. Start your collection, make a chart, tote them up on a whiteboard, because if you embrace the No's, it means you're getting closer. "No" is not a sign to stop. It's a sign to up the ante. Get those No's out of the way so when you're ready to launch, your groundwork is done.

Start promoting yourself in small ways. Do it for yourself, but don't get caught up in making sure it is perfect, or even if it will make money. About those cards: Get one that has your name and what you love, and start putting it out there. Give it a funny or catchy motto. We have a joke at our work, "Will do voice overs for food."

Just start nurturing the dream. Take a step, become a volunteer, find a mentor who is doing what you want to do. Never stop wondering about what is next. If we have a purpose, then it is our job to walk towards it and let it play out. Even if you say, "I don't know what it is I'm supposed to do." It doesn't matter, because it starts with what you love, and what you love is your seminal idea.

When I wanted to get back in radio, I didn't tell very many people because I knew they would think I was a just a dreamer. About the time my kids were almost out of the nest, I really had my doubts. Somehow I gave it my best shot and got back in the door. It started with an idea that I put into action by making a silly tape on my computer. The silly, made-up tape got me an actual interview which, of course, was a better tape. That got me another interview, and from that connection, I found Metro, where I applied for and got a job as a traffic reporter.

It still wasn't the "show" I imagined. That came later. When I got my own show, I lost the sponsors I needed to keep going. That gave me the opportunity to make the show even better. Now, my coaching partner and I are doing an entirely new call-in coaching show.

So, start with what you love. What are twenty things you love?

1
2
3
4
5
6
7
8
9
10
11
12
13
14
15
16
17
18
19
20

I also love public speaking, and I wanted to make a career of it. I asked women who were doing it, and they didn't always know how to help me. I read books by people doing what I wanted to do. I looked into courses and seminars offered by experts, but they were expensive. I found speakers who had a presence online and subscribed to their blogs.

The important thing was to find out what one has to do to be successful doing what you want to do. While I was doing all this hard work, I saw that people like me needed help. I vowed that, when I figured it out, I would show others how I did it.

Do some research and dream a little at first. Give yourself permission to wonder, allow yourself the freedom to think about what it will be like when you're living your dream. Then reduce it to the ridiculous. Find one thing you can do that propels you toward the fulfillment of your dream.

Tend to your dream. Think about nurturing. As parents, we nurture our children. We help them grow. We feed them and take care of them when they're sick. If you are a gardener, you understand what it means to nurture. If you are starting a plant from a seed, it needs water, sun, or not too much sun. You do your best to provide the ideal environment for it to grow. It's more than just planting - it's tending to it. I tended to my dream. Sound selfish? How can we help others, if we haven't nourished ourselves first?

Think about the little talk the flight attendants always give before the plane takes off. You know, the one no one listens to but if they did, they would pause when the attendant says, "Those of you with small children put your masks on first...then help your children with theirs." Doesn't that just make sense? I can help you breathe if I can breathe myself. If I take care of myself, I have more to offer my family, my friends, and my dream. Once the dream begins to flourish, then it begins nurturing me.

Surround yourself with people who can feel your heartache and who will encourage you to persevere. Be careful at first, and only tell people who are "for you." Don't cast your pearls before swine. Avoid telling "naysayers" what you are up to until you have been thinking about it awhile and can handle some negativity. Often their negative comments are a campaign for avoiding all risk and suffering.

Without heartache we don't grow. At times I've heard myself say: "Enough already! How much rejection can one girl take?" At that moment, I use my dream to spur me on. I find relief listening to podcasts of other coaches and then I think, "I can do this." The wounds heal, and I feel brave again, and I put my dream out there and help comes in unexpected ways.

"How much rejection can one girl take?"

My friend Jennifer was trying for a morning news job on a local radio station. She didn't get the job, but it opened the door for her to do what she really wanted. When she interviewed, she met some other people in a band who later fell in love with her saxophone playing and offered to let her be a part of some of their productions.

Through this connection, she also met a woman who shared her interests, and they produced a radio show together. At one of their events, she ended up meeting Mr. Right!

It all started because she was trying to get a job that would earn her enough to pay the rent and have a better life, but she didn't get it. She would tell you she got a whole lot more by not landing the job, and some of her good fortune spilled over into my cup.

I had a radio show that had been airing about six months when funds ran out. When bad economic times hit, I lost sponsors. I was devastated and felt like a failure. A dear friend encouraged me to fight for it. But being a single parent, I couldn't make time to market and sell advertising. So I let go. It broke my heart and I fell into a depression. I couldn't have known what would happen next.

Jennifer, now fully into making her dreams a reality, got a radio show going and asked me for some coaching audio segments. I recorded them and she played them on the air.

Soon after, I had lunch with my coach friend, Suzette, who had been a guest on my show, but who heard Jennifer's show and was reminded of her own segments on my show. She asked me if I was thinking of getting the show going again. I mentioned how sad I had been about losing the show, but that I couldn't sustain it on my own. She said, "You know, I have been really thinking about how much I loved being on your show and how fun it would be if we could revive it." How about that? Help came in an unexpected way.

As we began sharing ideas, our passion grabbed hold of us and we said, "Let's do it!" We didn't know how to do it at that point, but we were determined to figure it out. I couldn't muster the energy to try to do it again alone. We agreed to meet on a weekly basis to talk about the show.

We did a focus group and it went so well we couldn't believe it. We learned as we went. We spoke with someone who produced radio shows for Disney. He gave us some advice that I wasn't very happy about - he recommended we read *Crush It*, by Gary Vaynerchuk.

Based on Gary's formula, he suggested we do podcasts. Now, I wanted to do a radio show not a podcast. But because he was so gracious to meet with us via phone and offer advice I followed it. I bought the book, encouraged all my friends to do audio blogs, and finally Suzette and I started our own audio blogs. People seemed to like them and it gave us a lot of practice in working together for the upcoming show. I'm so glad I didn't blow him off because he didn't say what I wanted to hear! We made a website, posted our audio blogs, made a Facebook fan page. Finally, we launched a radio show called "Coffee With the Coaches."

Find your passion and start doing things around it that make you happy, make you smile, and scare you to death. It definitely improves the attitude.

Almost everything I am doing right now can be done without money. Don't let money or fear get in your way. Instead, ask for help and for information. What a time we live in where you can find free ways to get the job done that only a few years ago would have cost a fortune—enough to discourage loads of people.

"Remember to dream about the dream..."

Why bother with remembering the dream? Why open the door to heartache and disappointments? Why stir up the past passions only to face more hurt? Why? Because this too shall pass, and one day you will be looking back on your time as a single parent and you'll think "Now what?" What's next? Remember to dream about the dream while you're on our journey, even in the midst of a chaotic life.

The day will come when your kids are grown and on their own, and you forgot to remember what you loved. You may slide into depression. I know you're thinking, "No way. I will be doing the dance of joy when my responsibilities are over."

All of my time and energy went into parenting, survival, the day-to-day living, and then one day it was over. I was on my way to my dream, and I can't help but wonder how I would have coped had I not had things in place ahead of time. It doesn't take away the emptiness of having the kids raised, but it does help with the regret and resentment of not taking care of yourself.

Do yourself and your family a favor and remember what you love and think about what is next. What is your purpose? What makes you light up? What can you see yourself doing in your twilight years? How will you model for your children doing more than just surviving and making a living? What does it mean to really live?

What is your dream? I dare you to look at it, think about it, and value it. It is yours and it was given to you for your purpose here, and it is waiting for you to remember it. It is not selfish; it is self-full. It is you doing the thing that gives life to you. Kudos to you for being brave enough to look at and remember your dream. It makes me feel less lonely knowing there are others courageous enough to face their dreams.

Remember the dream, discover the dream, and give yourself permission to think about it. Dream about it; wonder about it. Nurturing the dream is finding a way to keep it real and alive, even if it has to be on hold for a while. You can read a book about it, take a class, find a group, volunteer. Nurturing the dream isn't about doing it right now. It is about keeping it alive, keeping the flame burning. It's about not giving up and not giving in. What have you been secretly wishing for? What is your dream?

"Remember the dream, discover the dream, and give yourself permission to think about it.

It's about not giving up and not giving in."

Just Wondering:

What does nurturing YOUR dream look like?

What is hard about it?

What is the risk?

What scares you about stepping out?

Are there others who can help you?

Would networking groups be a good connection for you?

Is there something you can do or somewhere you can volunteer to be doing what you love? I announced at horse shows and at the fair. It was huge fun.

Make a list of ten things you can do to nurture your dream.

Baby Steps

1

2

3

4

5

6

7

8

9

10

Prioritize the baby steps.

What tools do you need?

Can you do one a month?

Maybe one a week?

How about a daily activity that keeps you connected with your dream?

Start having fun doing what you love now, in the moment.

"Start having fun doing what you love now, in the moment."

14

Reducing it to the Ridiculous

"One spot at a time, spray, drop the paper towel, and use your toe to mop."

--Cousin Donna

Nurturing the dream is like planting a seed and helping it grow. It takes weeks to grow and months to mature. In the intervening time, you think about it, visit it, check on it, water it, and most of all wonder what will happen. Nurturing it is keeping it alive and respecting your purpose. Nurturing isn't about timing. It is what you do in the midst of timing, good or bad. It is what keeps us going when times get tough, wondering what is next.

Maybe you love what you do and are happy with it. Does it make life a little easier doing something you love? Is it what you want to do forever? Or are you thinking about making a change? Nurturing the dream is giving it a place to grow and sprout wings.

I moved into a brand new mobile home. The kitchen and dining room were huge, and the linoleum was white. Cousin Donna came for a visit, and knowing me like she did, she grabbed the glass cleaner and a paper towel and said, "This is what you have to do. Every time you spill or see a spill, just grab the spray, squirt it, then drop the paper towel on it. Use your toe to move it around and voila! It's clean! Don't wait until you have time to mop the whole floor, because it won't happen."

Thus, "toe mopping" was born. Reduce it to the ridiculous - small baby steps to help us get through. Looking at the big picture can be overwhelming, in any scenario. But when you break it down to steps, the process seems more manageable.

Life can get overwhelming, and it is easy to get lost in all the "to do" and lose sight of the "want to." Taking steps toward your dream keeps it real. Just baby steps. Take the big picture of your dream, which may seem overwhelming and impossible, and break it into small doable parts. Ask yourself, "What is one step, one thing I can do today toward my dream?"

Set aside a certain amount of time each day or each week for dream maintenance. For a long time, my fear kept me thinking about it, talking about it, and that was great, exciting, fun. I loved thinking about it.

Taking action was another thing. When I knew there was a job opening and I wanted to take in a resume or CD,I would choke. I was scared to death, and a little embarrassed. What if they laughed me out of town? I would ask my friends to hold me accountable. "Did you call today?" I would say, "No, but I promise I'll do it tomorrow." Sometimes it took every thing I had to muster the courage to take a step. Remember, I got my share of "No's" and guess what? It didn't kill me.

I took on the saying, "Fake it till you make it." I had to believe and go on pure faith at times. Yes, I got discouraged. Yes, I cried, Yes, I cursed. It was all part of the journey and adventure. I had stories to tell friends about who I met and what I saw. This was scary exciting. I kept thinking, "What if I don't try? I'll never know if I could have made it."

I didn't think I could live with not trying. I didn't want my tombstone to read, "She was just too scared." Or worse, "What if." I want to be an example, pave the way. I want to live in "You can do it!" Sometimes people are raised being told they can do anything. I think that is a disservice, because we all can't do everything. There are things we are good at, though, and there are things we are passionate about.

Along with all the wonderful stories of people who have made it against all odds, there are stories of people who "fell into" a great opportunity. There are people who want to do or be something, and they're no good at it. My coach wanted to play pro football, but when he was getting ready for college, he got an injury that put him out of the game. He loved football, but he also loved speaking. He is now speaking and doing his best to raise money to buy an NFL team.

"I think that is the danger in "hoping" for one thing and one thing only."

My partner in coaching tells a story about a woman who is a terrible singer. Her mother led her to believe she is a wonderful singer. You can imagine how that turned out. We've all seen American Idol, and the singers hope beyond hope they make it. And when they don't, they're angry and crushed. For some it opens other doors, for others, it was just another letdown. I think that is the danger in "hoping" for one thing and one thing only. If it doesn't come true, we're devastated.

When we wonder, and accept the adventure and journey, it can lead us to somewhere we never expected and to something we like even more. It can show us the way to jobs and careers we didn't know existed. The dream is the driving force. What we do with it and our attitude about following it will guide our steps toward fulfilling it.

"The dream, what we love, will fuel us. It fills our cup, and then we're able to give to and love others."

Some people have more than one thing they love, more than one goal. Maybe one will be a hobby. Here's the thing that drives me. When we are doing what we love, we're content in our lives. We love better, we give better, we are living our purpose and that gives us a sense of fulfillment. I want to give my time, money, and resources. It's important to me, but if I'm miserable, working a job I hate, even if I make a lot of money, I won't be all that great to be around.

When we love what we do, we love our lives. We have found something we love in spite of a difficult life, children with disorders, or caring for an elderly parent. The dream, what we love, will fuel us. It fills our cup, and then we're able to give to and love others.

We've all been around people who hate their jobs and hate their life, and they seem to hate everybody. Finding your purpose, discovering your dream, and taking steps toward living it in some way, is the greatest gift you can give this world. It is a gift to you, your joy in it is a gift to others, and the world was waiting for you, because it knew all along you were meant for this.

Some people don't believe they deserve anything good. They think it is selfish to live what you love. Some people even think we are supposed to be miserable - that our purpose here is to suffer. At times I've almost been convinced myself that we're meant to be miserable. But here is the question I ask:

How miserable do we have to be to make God happy?

Not everyone is going to think about, let alone pursue, his or her dream. It's sad! I want to encourage everyone I encounter to live their dream. Find what you love and give enthusiastically.

Many people give because they "should." Some give begrudgingly. In the Bible it says that God loves a cheerful giver. This is so deep. What does it take for us to be cheerful givers? Confidence that we have enough to share. Faith that there will be enough for us. Belief that what we are giving will make a difference, no matter how big or small. A heart of cheerful giving comes from a loving heart. When I'm living my dream, feeling a sense of worth (like what I do matters,) then I love better, and I give better - in fact, I give cheerfully.

"Find something that feeds your soul. It isn't selfish; it is self-full."

Many kids go to college to be what their parents want them to be. People take certain jobs because they "should." People give up on dreams all the time and it breaks my heart. I hear people shatter the dreams of others with their negativity. It hurts my soul. We all have different things we love. At my workshops, when we all write or say twenty things we love, no two lists are ever the same. We all have our unique desires and dreams. They are ours, even if other people call them silly, or call us dreamers. Take the job you "should," but make a plan to live your dream.

Life happens; single parenting happens; dreams get hijacked. Don't let them die. Keep them alive, one month, one year, ten years. It's never too late to live what you love, be it a job, or a hobby. Find something that feeds your soul. It isn't selfish; it is self-full. It gives you what you need so you can give others what they need. It is life.

What is something that feels overwhelming to you?

What is one small step you can take?

And another?

Before you know it, you are well underway, and it is no longer so daunting.

Now there are some projects that are so overwhelming and you can't possibly take time to work on them because you have so much going on. In fact, you don't even want to do it because once you start it, you feel an obligation to finish. Sometimes a small step will be giving the project to someone who in fact has the time and wants to do it.

Throw it away.

Give it away.

Take it away.

Sweet relief.

What is one project you can chuck? Sometimes we just fill our time up with things that are meaningless and not even something we want to do, and yet they have a hold on us. Some times projects are nothing more than a diversion to keep us from what we love, our dreams and desires. We can just think about our dreams but surely we don't have any time to work towards them because of all our unfinished projects. Sometimes we're just trying to stay busy.

But when we free up our time and let go of some projects, we create space for new things - for what we really love. We can just think about our dreams but surely we don't have any time to work towards them because of all our unfinished projects. Chuck some, I dare you.

Another aspect to taking steps is that the way to our dream can be lonely. There are people who want us to get there faster, slower, or not at all. Some people get jealous, or think you can't do what you love and still keep them as friends. Sometimes people just don't seem to understand.

Can you face the loneliness? Realize it may be for a time. I want connection and community, and when I feel like I'm going it alone, it's really hard. It feels like I'm doing something wrong. Leadership can be lonely, and when you are taking the steps to your dream, it is a place of leadership. Don't take it as a sign you're on the wrong path.

Remember Frodo in *The Lord of the Rings*? When he set out to destroy the ring, all the elfin, dwarf, and other leaders joined with him. It was so beautiful, but then some of them came up with "ring-envy" and tried to get the ring away from Frodo. So he went off alone to accomplish his mission and ended up in a castle tied to a slab of rock. His good friend Sam showed up and carried him out. He thought he had to go it alone and was willing to do so for the mission, but discovered he had a friend that could help.

Loneliness is part of the journey. Try to embrace it and make the most of it, rather than indulge it with sadness and pity.

Toe mopping, reducing it to the ridiculous, and baby steps are key words to help you move toward what you love. The big picture can be too much and seem too impossible, but step by step, you will make it.

"Toe mopping, reducing it to the ridiculous, and baby steps are key words to help you move toward what you love."

Just Wondering:

Do you fall into any of the categories that deny you the ability to live your dream?

Selfish, suffering, not worthy?

If so, which one?

Tell me about it. How did this attitude come about?

What can you do or say to give yourself permission to change that?

What is your dream? Okay, what is an idea you have thrown around and wished could happen?

What does reducing it to the ridiculous look like for you?

What would one step toward the dream be?

Is it scary? Good. Ask for a friend to hold you accountable or hire a life coach.

Have you experienced loneliness on your journey? What was it like? Did it make you want to stop and settle?

15

This Too Shall Pass

"Life must be lived as a play."

--Plato

Reducing things to the ridiculous, taking baby steps, and toe mopping are starting points for those who wish to live the dream. In the midst of all this dreaming, life's events still happen. They beckon us away. Reality calls, and we have to respond to its exigencies, but this too shall pass.

Since my youngest child has graduated, I have the time to reflect on some of the more intense times we went through as a family.. In the midst of the crises, all I could see was the here and now. It never occurred to me that "this too shall pass." I was so caught up in the need of moment that I couldn't anticipate getting through the situation, and that one day I would be looking back on it. I took my responsibility as a parent very seriously, and I worried a lot whether I was handling things correctly. I so wanted to be right and to do things the right way. It was all consuming and it felt like it was going to go on forever.

Now I look back and it's over. I have finished carrying that huge burden alone. Yes, they are still my children and they have struggles, but they are adults. I wonder if things would have been better had I realized this was just a moment in time and it would pass? I'm not feeling regret. But I am wondering, if I could have saved myself a few gray hairs had I realized it is all part of a temporary, fading process. I worried about the long-term ramifications of each decision and thought that I could lose them, or do irreparable damage, if I chose wrongly. What if I had thought differently and realized these incidents were not simply teachable moments, but also passing fancies?

"It never occurred to me that "this too shall pass.""

I worried so much about my own inadequacies. I worried I might be too lenient or too tough. I worried that if one of my kids got angry and became distant that I would lose him or her. I often chose to be right at the expense of relationship with my child. I worried: Is this too much or too little? Interestingly, each decision I thought to be the moment of truth at the time turned out to be brought about by a conflict I cannot even remember. It all seems so important in the moment, but the moment passes and with it goes the weighty issue. Yes, this too shall pass. Every hurt, frustration, disappointment, and struggle fades away and in the end we are left with relationship.

At my son's graduation, I felt both sadness and joy. I was happy my kids made it ready to face life, but I was sad that the daily parenting part was over. As I looked around the gym at other parents saying goodbye, I felt like I had missed out on much of the fun of parenting because of my unshared responsibility.

I wasn't able to run around with a camera at every one of my kid's events. I didn't even own a camera, partly because I was in the era between digital and film. Digital cameras were expensive, but everyone knew film was becoming obsolete. Out-of-date notwithstanding, film was expensive to develop. I didn't get to make cupcakes and go on field trips because I worked. I couldn't take a day off because I was the sole breadwinner. I didn't get to have girls' night with the other mothers because I didn't have someone to stay home with the kids while I went out and played. I didn't get a babysitter because I couldn't afford one.

We didn't go on vacations or trips, but we did live on a farm near a beach. I did get to have a lot of kids over, and I would be as creative as possible to feed them because I wanted them at my house. I wanted my kids' friends to feel welcome at our home. Sometimes it was tough when it was the end of the month and the cupboards were bare. If my kids wanted friends over, I didn't want food to be a barrier. Kids are all about snacks, so I found a way. For example, did you know kids actually like uncooked ramen crunched up and put in a serving bowl? Who knew?

"...I wouldn't trade the good, bad, and ugly for anything."

But now, suddenly, I was free to pursue my dream and my life changed drastically overnight. I had time on my hands. I was able to jump into the process because I was planning ahead, but I was surprised how guilty I still felt for not being enough for my children. I had to be realistic about my kids' upbringing, in that we struggled in many ways.

Nevertheless, I wouldn't trade the good, bad, and ugly for anything. It made our family what it is, and we are better for it. For example, I saw an unusual maturity that developed in each of us. We survived difficulties that made us humble, appreciative, and compassionate toward others who suffer. And our difficulties brought out the best in other people. We have known the gift of true friends who love, listen, and encourage. We have been believed in and hoped for.

There were people who sat with me and let me vent my spleen about my troubles. The same people brainstormed with me when I was optimistically creative. I am so grateful for those noble souls who looked straight at me with a twinkle in their eyes and said, "You are going to make it," and "This too shall pass," not in a "Good luck, lady" way, but in lock step with me, providing community and friendship.

One of those supportive people was my baby sister (so much more mature than I) who, when I felt like my life was about to fall apart because I felt like I couldn't do it on my own anymore, said, "Laurie, stop it. You are the mother your kids need. You give them all they need. They know you love them." She was so right, and I was free not just because they were on their own, but because they could look back as young adults and reflect that they were loved well, even though there were rough patches in their childhoods.

Now I am looking to my future. I nurtured the dream, I took some risks, I made some headway, and now I can begin to pursue the dream fully. I know that I worried I would be too old by the time they graduated. But they say fifty is the new thirty!

I remember when I made the choice to not date until my kids were grown. We had been through enough, and I didn't want to be the one to cause them any more grief. When you live on an island, just dating for the fun of it wasn't a possibility. It's the small-town way; everyone knows your business. I knew that if I dated and my heart got broken, it would affect my parenting and my kids would be cheated again. It sort of felt like a gift I could give my kids. But then the truth hit me: I would be over fifty when my youngest graduated!

"...fifty is the new thirty!"

Events in each of our lives pass and we hold on to a memory. But our dreams never fade. We each have stories about missed opportunities that only came knocking once. But our dreams never really go away. They are waiting. Does that seem possible? That would mean it would never be too late to pursue one's dream.

Yep, that's it. We're never too old, too weak, not smart enough, or handicapped by our past. Remember, you're hearing that from me, the woman who was sure life had passed her by, dealt her a losing hand, and felt guilty about not being enough for the ones who trusted her and depended on her.

A good friend is 62 and wants to be a lawyer, and although that may seem outrageous to some people, I believe he is going to do it. What do you love? What dream is waiting for you? Are you too exhausted to try again? Are you afraid you are going to run into another dead end?

I remember when I tried for yet one more radio job, and I was in the top three of the final cut. I thought, "If I don't get this job I am so DONE." What a ridiculous thought that was. This was my dream! I didn't get the job, but my friends had a pity party for me, and after a few days I pulled myself together and tried again.

We've all said it and heard others say, "I just don't want to get my hopes up." Another oldie, but a goodie: "I just need to lower my expectations." What tripe. What balderdash! That stuff floats up out of the deep well of self-protection that keeps me small and safe, but numb. The deep pain of disappointment should not be blunted because it confirms how much what I love is just that: What I love.

I don't want to live in the place where I miss my calling in order to avoid disappointment and heartache. Livin' safe ain't livin'. It's knowing heartache that makes us compassionate and disappointment that makes us realize our humanity. I want to learn from all these things, and I am willing to feel the disappointment as I pursue the joy. I wouldn't miss a moment of it for anything. I don't want to waste my life avoiding pain.

When my daughter celebrated her second wedding anniversary, a coworker asked how old she was. The coworker remarked that her age was way too young to get married. She said that kids haven't lived enough life at that age. I said, "Well, maybe most kids haven't, but mine have lived several life times! They have a maturity beyond their years because of what we've been through together."

That was when I realized that I didn't need to feel guilty for what they didn't get or what we didn't have. I wanted to rejoice that so many of the life lessons people get later in life, my kids experienced early on, with me to walk through it with them. When I remember to focus on what I'm grateful for, I can honestly look at the gifts my children have and be happy for the grief and angst that got us to where we are today.

What if everything we went through was a gift in disguise? What if it all meant something wonderful in the end? What if the struggles and trials spur us on to greatness? There are so many what if's like this that can empower our journey. What if you are right where you need to be for the "what's next" in your life? I didn't want to be that single mom. It wasn't my passion or my dream, but it has become my gift, and I am grateful.

"What if everything we went through was a gift in disguise?"

"This, too, shall pass" is not just a promise for unpleasant things. My regrets nudge up against the things I miss about raising a family, and I realize they will never be babies again, never have a first day at school, never dress for the prom. Now it really is over, and I miss all the action. As I write, football season is getting underway and I'm sad. I miss the camaraderie with the other parents. I miss squinting at the artificially illuminated field to pick out my son's number, the pride when he made a great block. Life is different - no visiting the school and running into friends.

The pathways of my life are changing, and I made a transition, but it doesn't make me miss it all any less. My circles are different, and life is taking a new and exciting turn. I'm happy, but there is a certain sadness when I hear other parents talk of gearing up for school and sports. It's a relief financially to not be buying school supplies this year, but I miss having all the teenagers in my home. I will see them when I see my kids, but it's different. I loved raising my children and interacting with other kids, but my world is now full of adults. So there is sadness mixed with relief.

It was an enriching adventure, and I am so glad I didn't miss it. But I'm also grateful that I began reviving my dream and taking steps in the midst of raising kids, because I cannot imagine where I would be without the dream. Have you ever seen that poster of hundreds of penguins with just one smack in the middle of the crowd with a red bow tie and colorful party hat and the caption that says, "I just gotta be me!" I love that poster, but I hate it too, because I always identify with the hundreds of clones. Who will see me? I'm just like every other penguin. I'm not special or different. How do I stand out and who will notice me? My friend challenged me to look at that poster differently. She said it was true that all those look-alike penguins are just like me. Strugglers, we are together in this journey.

It reminded me of a story in the book Me to We. The authors, Marc and Craig Kielburger, share a story about how zebras move together in a wave and produce a unique kind of camouflage. They don't match the browns and greens of the savannah environment. No, their camouflage is that you cannot tell where one animal ends and another begins. But if one of those zebras were to wear a red bow tie, it would be curtains because the predator's attention would be drawn to the one who stands out. So being a community is not insignificant but, rather, life-giving. Together we make it and together we live. Alone we can be eaten alive or wither in isolation. We need each other.

Sometimes we want to be unnoticed because of our shame, and we push people away to prove we are unlovable, but isolation is death. I have a friend who got so fed up with people he assumed he hated them. It took years to discover that his disillusionment was a result of his deep longing to love and be loved by people. Are you so troubled by people that you think you could do without them? The alternative, isolation, is worse than the grief that others cause us. What about the pain of disappointment in people? Well, it seems that this too shall pass.

If we remember this too shall pass when our kids are struggling, it's easier to encourage them. There were times when they were frustrated or sad and I was, too. I naturally tried to find ways to ease their pain—something I could never do completely. I certainly acknowledged the reality of their hurt. They were not deluded about feeling disappointment. I looked for an opportunity to empower them by telling them the positive aspects of a situation rather than merely getting caught up in the tragedy of it. I didn't promise something I couldn't deliver, like telling them everything would be okay, but I helped them find a truth they could hang on to.

It was heart wrenching when I had to drop my daughter off at daycare and she cried. But perhaps the guilt that followed was more about the parent than the child. My sister and I talked about the fact that I can just feel bad and cry, too (when I get to the car,) or I can tell her, "You are going to have so much fun, make new friends, and before you know it, I'll be back." Empowerment.

I went to the car and cried anyway, but we have the power to let go of our fears and not impose them on our children. We can be the "cruise director" for their thoughts about difficult situations. If we resist the urge to indulge the fear and push through to the positive possibilities, it benefits all of us. Daycare? Well, that too has passed, but the life skill to see the blessing in what we didn't see coming will put us in good stead for the rest of our lives.

I received grace when I reached out to others who struggled with the same things I did. I hope I offered grace to others as well. It is futile, and even arrogant, to try to do it perfectly. I never became super mom and I could not do it all. Unless I acknowledged that I was needy, I was in no position to receive the gift from someone who could do for me what I could not do for myself. We all need grace, understanding, validation, and love. This too shall pass, but in the midst when we are offered a hand—or offer a loving hand to others—we discover the blessing that is community, and perseverance becomes possible.

Just Wondering:

Do you find yourself isolating and retreating from life?

Under what circumstances do you isolate and/or retreat?

What can you find to do that will keep you in a relationship?

Keep you in the game?

Do you have other single parent friends?

Is there a group you could join for support?

What does it feel like to think about this just being a passing thing?

Does thinking about what you love bring you joy?

Are you struggling with depression?

Is it hard to get out of bed?

Is it intolerable to face another day?

If you are struggling with those types of issues, seek help. I know counseling can be expensive, but look for resources. Sometimes a church will have a counselor you can see.

Take care of you. Get back in the game. The kids need you. We need you. This, too, shall pass. Together, we can find the courage to face tomorrow. Let others in, so they can support you. Ask for help.

What are you looking forward to when this is all said and done?

What does it mean to you to be in it, rather than wishing a situation away? Is there a situation where you can apply this idea?

How does it feel?

What will you do differently?

16

Living the Dream

"We all have dreams. But in order to make dreams come into reality, it takes an awful lot of determination, dedication, self-discipline, and effort."

--Jesse Owens

Things change, but while we're in the midst of it we don't notice. Other people told me to enjoy my kids, because their childhoods go by so fast. I did enjoy them, but I never got the "go by fast" part. One minute I had two boys in diapers, and the next minute these same two boys were driving automobiles. Where did the in between go? I can't remember details. Why didn't I memorize every conversation and savor every moment in their company? Why am I so inept at being present in the process? It seems like when I am in the midst of a journey, no matter whether unpleasant or glorious, I want to skip to the destination, the payoff.

"I want the quick fix and I want to win the lottery."

I'm a sucker for get-rich-quick schemes. I heard an interview about a "how-to" program and it made me want to order it. I read an email about how to find ten thousand dollars in 72 hours, and I followed the link to buy the secret. I want the quick fix and I want to win the lottery. I want to be rescued. Oh, I dream and wonder, but I still want it quicker. I want the McDonald's fast-food version of my dream: When I'm hungry, I want it now. Andy, my chef friend, tells me not to rush the best stuff. It needs to cook slowly and the right way. Don't rush the process.

Too often we dream of quiche, but settle for scrambled eggs. Scrambled eggs taste good enough, and they are easy to prepare. But egg lovers know quiche is better. It is also more complicated and takes longer. It's worth waiting for, but I want my eggs now. I don't like process. This puzzles a chef like Andy, who knows the journey to the most delicious is as fulfilling and enjoyable as eating it.

"Chef Andy tells me not to rush the best stuff."

I wanted the revival of my dream to be smooth so I could get to the dream part. Instead, I have encountered frustrations like financial issues, computer glitches, car breakdowns, and I never get to the glorious finish. I end up feeling like I am banging my head against a wall, but what did I expect? I expected calm seas and pleasant sailing that seldom represent my reality. Oh sure, sometimes things fall in my lap, but most times it is one small step forward and then what seems like ten steps backward.

Something has to help me over the hump of discouragement. First and most important is the support of friends and family who believe in me when I don't believe in myself. Second, when I am frustrated and stuck, I try to do something for other people. Taking the focus off myself makes me feel better, and hopefully blesses someone else. Third, I listen to people who have the ability to motivate me. Fourth, I do a little self talk in which I find the positive in even the most negative circumstances. I don't pretend to feel something I don't, and if I feel, say, frustrated, I have to acknowledge it.

I have enough experience to know that many times it can ultimately be a blessing when things don't go the way I planned. If something thwarts me from the outside, well, I can't change that. But I can anticipate the benefits of new, unplanned directions that I receive. The most obvious question is, "What did I learn here that is going to help me in the future?" My path just changed. I don't know where this is leading, but I can be hip to it. Sounds like an adventure, doesn't it?

Stuck in traffic.

Going to be late?

I wonder what might come of this?

What can I learn?

When I was in my twenties, I was facing a difficult time and feeling very sad. My aunt told me to be sad, then get over it. Give yourself permission to be sad, frustrated, or disappointed about daily setbacks, but then move on. If you struggle with depression, by all means get help. I'm not suggesting flipping a switch that turns sadness on and off, but the advice is pretty sound.

"Give yourself permission to be sad, frustrated, or disappointed about daily setbacks, but then move on."

I begin by acknowledging what is true: I am sad and frustrated. But it's also true that I won't always be sad and frustrated. Part of the reason for this is that my experience has left me wiser. I can learn. And if I can learn, I can change. And if I can change, I can change for the better.

My loss can make me better. This seems elementary, but all coaches know this: winning may be more fun, but you learn a lot more when you lose. When you finally do experience victory, it's all the sweeter because you now have the gift of perspective (you know where you came from and what it means) rather than the albatross of entitlement (the world owes me).

Dreaming doesn't mean things are going to turn out the way I envision them. Some people "indulge" in a dream as a way of controlling their environments. Like spoiled children, they fall down kicking and screaming and holding their breath if they don't get their way. Then they walk away and say, "Well, that didn't work," and refuse to dream again.

Dreaming is part of being fully human. So is disappointment and failure. Sometimes I forget that my big dream is more general, and so when the specific steps to the big dream are thwarted (course correction) it doesn't mean the dream must end. Real dreams are full of possibilities that exceed even our wildest expectations.

To hope is a positive thing, but when we pin our hopes on one thing without being open to greater possibilities, we become mistrustful and withholding. Trust, on the other hand, allows us to persevere through the experience of being shot down because we're willing to do whatever it takes. It doesn't have to be our way or the highway. We can also give and love in the midst of our suffering, because we know we won't always be in a state of suffering.

One way I show trust is to celebrate the small victories. I really depend on my computer. So when I started to have computer problems that brought my progress to a screeching halt, I wanted to throw in the towel and toss the laptop out the window. However, my coach reminded me to ask for help, so I asked my coworkers if they had any ideas. Within minutes, I had a very viable solution. Imagine that! Other people have had the same problems I have! This simple solution really uncomplicated my life, so I was really and truly grateful. I wanted to dance! High fives all around! Hooray! Score: Human Race 1, Computers 0.

Let others help.

Brain storm ideas.

Use your community.

Brainstorming is so nourishing to our dreams! To have a brainstorming session, put out the problem, issue, or situation. Open the floor to suggestions. Keep the answers short and to the point. Remind everyone this is a suggestion not a "you should do this" kind of group. It's a quick process, just a couple of minutes. The person who put out the issue writes down all the suggestions. Very likely, most of the suggestions will be things you have already thought about.

The beauty is that all the suggestions will spur your thoughts and creativity. When the brainstorming is over, debrief. Ask the person writing the ideas down what grabbed them. And oh yeah, no judgments in this part of the process. "We can't do that," and "We tried that already and it didn't work," are banished from this exercise. It is an easy, fun, creative activity

If brainstorming nourishes our dreams, there are plenty of toxins out there waiting to crush them. To remind myself and my friends that our dreams are fragile, I have a set of "gremlin" finger puppets, so ugly they are funny. I keep them around and hand them out as a reminder that we each have a dream-destroying gremlin inside us working to ridicule our ideas and frighten us into abandoning that which we envision.

The gremlin sort of has a life of its own and scrapes and scratches to survive as if its own existence will expire, if we ever achieve success. If we can only recognize the presence and the voice of this pest within, we can subvert his wicked designs.

"How do I recognize this gremlin within?"

How do I recognize this gremlin within? It is the voice that says, "Who are you to help others when your life is a mess?"

"See, your doubt is a sign you are not to follow your dream."

"You are not creative."

"You will make a fool of yourself."

"You can't take that big of a risk."

We need friends to loan us their strength when the gremlin threatens to undo us. We need to show we remember the positive things about our dreams by enumerating the best and the beautiful when the negative shadows fall around us. The best and the beautiful is what each of us knows, I mean really knows. Like "Who am I really? I am smart, creative, loved. I contribute."

I ask my friends how they see me. They speak truth. They are often willing to use bigger, bolder words about the true me than I dare to when the naysaying voices speak up. What they share about me feels like extravagant gifts wrapped in beautiful paper and bows. Positive truth is a gift. It may seem strange at first, but reveling in it banishes the gremlin. A friend of mine keeps a file of notes and cards other people send her with compliments in them. When she's down, she just pulls one out of her file to get a sweet dose of compliments to giver her a boost.

Every creative person struggles with gremlins. The fact that the pests bug creative types shows that gremlins are dirty little liars - nothing more than petty leeches that suck our time and energy and leave us lethargic about pursuing good things. They vaporize our passion and convince us that we had none in the first place, or the voice that says how do we the unworthies dare to be passionate about anything? Nasty, nasty, pernicious little devils, these gremlins. Defy them. If you didn't have something worth sharing, you wouldn't have to worry about gremlins.

You can defy the "odds." I just watched a video of a man, Nick Vujicic, with no arms and no legs, speaking to people about living their dreams. Even without arms and legs, you have no excuse for giving in to the gremlins.

"Every creative person struggles with gremlins."

Maybe living your dream is about changing jobs, starting your own business, or just making changes to your current situation. Remember to reduce it to the ridiculous; don't take on the whole big picture. It will take many baby steps to get to your goal. You know you may have to keep your day job, and it may seem like you are never going to get your dream, but just keep moving toward it. There are many books available to help you start your own business; there are also people who have done it who would mentor you to get you started.

The transition can be tough because as single parents we have limited time, money, and energy. Take baby steps and see what unfolds. There are programs like the Small Business Association and some local programs you can search out that will help you get a loan to start a business. Find people who are doing what you want to do and ask them to mentor you. If it is a direct competition, then maybe find someone in a different community or state who can help you out.

"Remember to reduce it to the ridiculous;..."

Use your resources; don't go it alone. If people give you negative feedback, such as, "With this economy, you would be smart to just keep doing what you're doing and forget any risk," thank them and move on. See what nuggets you can take from their advice, but don't stop moving forward.

I have friends who created a business just as the economy was crashing, and they have been extremely successful. Their environmentally friendly cleaning products, Elf Naturals, have made it on the shelves of huge chain stores, and we're all so excited that they're securing their futures.

Dream living takes some coordination and organization, but it will happen. Sometimes it changes directions, takes a different shape. Maybe you wanted to be a singer, but you're really a songwriter.

Maybe you wanted to be a football player and you're too old now, but you can still revive the dream. Not to suggest that younger players gang tackle you until you bones break, but imagine what it might look like to follow the path and see where it takes you.

Get support if you'll be making a transition from a job t o a dream. Maybe your dream is a hobby, like baking cakes for fun. Think about how your dream can play out. Start small: one step, one cake, one season. See where the venture leads. Evaluate each step along the way. Invite friends to be a part of it. Expect that they may get scared for you or even jealous. Try to recognize that and don't let it stop you.

Dreaming can be scary, and so many people dance around it. They don't want to say what their dreams are. They default to the easy, routine stuff they know they can do. Some people just run scared, even when they know better. What makes us so afraid of our dreams, passions, or desires?

Take action NOW. My coach, Patrick Snow, advises that we take one dumb step after another. The key is taking the step. It's easy to worry about doing it wrong and thus never doing it at all. I walk the fine line of rushing into something and being afraid to take a step when I know I am ready.

"Start small: one step,
one cake,
one season."

My friend Marley heard a report about how the way we think affects our wealth. She says people who are in poverty think about today, poor people think about tomorrow, the middle class think ahead one to five years, and the wealthy think decades ahead.

I know for me, when I was at poverty level, I couldn't think ahead. It was too much to bear and felt like death. As things get better, I'm able to look farther into the future, dream and wonder. Respect where you are and know that this too will pass. There will come a day you will be well on your way to your dream.

Let's take the step together. Let's be ridiculous together; then we can laugh about it later. I want to leave a legacy. I want to live on as someone who encouraged others. I want to encourage others on the radio, and so I will take the risk.

Just Wondering:

What terrifies you about your dream?

What is the worst thing that could happen if you pursued your dream?

What is the best thing that could happen?

What fine line do you walk? Waiting? Rushing in?

What is the risk you are afraid to take?

What are the "what if's" you are dealing with?

Who is your support team?

Barbara Sherr talks about having Allies. After reading about this in one of Sherr's books, a friend created a "Gallery of Heroes." It's a group of people, dead, alive, made up, or real. You may know them, or maybe you just wish you knew them.

These are people who have influenced you and who you would like to have around your table to share in dialogue. I chose someone very funny, very serious, someone encouraging, and someone I just loved. I have also chosen celebrities, neighbors, friends, even dead people and characters of literary fiction.

Who would be in your gallery?

Who is your hero?

Who do you look up to?

Who do you admire?

Who has done something you respect?

Who would you love to have coffee with if you won the chance to meet with any one of your choice?

What questions would you ask?

Who do you know who has done something similar to what you want to do?

What are three questions you would put before your gallery?

What do you think their responses would be?

Where are you in the process of your dream?

What is getting in your way?

What life situations are you dealing with that keep your dream on hold?

What are you doing to nurture the dream while life is happening?

What are you wondering about your dream?

What do you see as the challenges ahead?

Dreaming the dream is not the last stage of the dream; it is the dream. It is the journey. In dreaming, you are already taking steps; you are already putting yourself out there. You have already begun researching. You know what you know, and you are on the path. You are now collecting allies for the adventure.

"The key is taking the step. There will come a day you will be well on your way to your dream."

You are on your way and whether it takes a week, a month, a year or ten years, you are on the path; you are living the adventure, dreaming the dream, and reviving your spirits. You will have bad days; you will feel frustrated; you will be tempted to bail.

Know this, and accept it, but remind yourself this is all going to happen. It is all part of the process. What is different, about life before the dream and life during the dream, is that the dream keeps you going. It gives you a focus; it gives you a place to go when times get tough. It energizes you and gives you strength to get through the day, the moment, life.

17

Mentoring

"To the world you may be just one person but to one person you may be the world."

--Anonymous

Being a single mom, I found much joy whenever I could reach out to make another person's load a little lighter. My job with Big Brother/ Big Sister brought new life and meaning to me. Being involved in that organization's mission brought home the colossal influence of mentoring. Seeing how life-giving relationships with those farther along life's path could be to children highlighted my own need and longing to be mentored both personally and professionally.

For many years, I struggled to figure out how to become a public speaker. I asked public speakers to mentor me. What I discovered wasn't so much an unwillingness to help, but a self-awareness on their part that they did not know how to mentor someone like me. Always looking for a good opportunity, I signed up when I heard that a large church was offering well-publicized workshops on mentoring.

When it became apparent during the session that the emphasis on imparting knowledge became central to the leader's definition of mentoring, I felt confused. So I raised my hand and asked, "What about being a friend?" The response was that mentoring is about leading and teaching minus friendship. It seemed to be a gaping flaw that the presenter was ignoring the vital importance of relationship as the overarching theme in mentoring. There are different forms of mentoring. Job mentoring places priority on instruction. Life coaching places priority on helping define dreams and goals. The Bible gives many examples and underlines the importance of discipleship. There are many books written on mentoring, coaching, and discipleship.

I believe the foundation for mentoring is relationship. Caring brings about trust. Howard Hendricks, a seminary professor, speaker and author, spent his life training and preparing people who wanted to become leaders, pastors, and teachers. The heart of his message was "They won't care what you know until they know that you care."

Building relationships means showing you care in concrete ways. In Big Brother/Big Sister, I saw the impact that the "Bigs" had when they played basketball or the guitar, read books or magazines aloud, played board games or just "hung out" with their "Littles." Each month I spoke with the Bigs, the Littles and their parents, and we all discovered the change that was happening when relationship was the basis of time spent together.

"I believe the foundation for mentoring is relationship."

"'They won't care what you know until they know that you care.'"

I've had several mentors in my life. Some were assigned to me, but some were my choice. Some have remained a part of my life, others only for a season. I once had a great time when I led a workshop for a group who wanted to start a mentoring program in their church. I discovered that women want to be mentored, but lack the confidence to mentor. It was obvious all of them had something to offer because it was coming through to me in their willingness to offer me relationship. All have something to impart, so how can we be mentored and mentor at the same time?

More than merely offering my knowledge of a skill, I have actually mentored people to sew, garden, speak and do various other things in which I have experience and know-how. They began by wanting to learn, but we also became friends as we spent time together, working on projects and talking about issues. Don't we all want to offer what we have to our friends?

Mentoring is friendship. Mentoring is a gift you give of yourself. If someone wants to learn to sew, we sew for hours, living those hours together. If they want to garden, we pull weeds. If they want to learn how to keep a house clean and tidy...well, they probably have to find someone else! A mentor doesn't have to be the leading expert or do it perfectly. We just share what we know. When we build trust and we believe in others and they believe in us, we will be able to share hard truths on the way and help each other grow.

I have a friend who wanted to be in a mentoring program at her church. They matched older women with younger women. She was matched with a wonderful woman whom she admired greatly. But the older woman had an agenda. She believed my friend wore too much make up and wanted to change that. That relationship was doomed from the beginning.

I put together a small book once that was actually a bunch of colorful pieces of paper on a big metal ring called "What if Mentoring Was...." Each page had a suggestion prompting creative thoughts about what mentoring could be. Some examples were:

A phone call

Encouragement

A listening ear

Offering a ride or a meal

Believing in someone who can't believe in themselves yet

Having a cup of coffee

Crying together

Sharing dessert

Going for a walk

Babysitting

Spending time with a friend's child

Loving a friend's child

Showing up during a difficult time and not giving advice

Being a friend, even if for a day

Never underestimate the power of mentoring.

When I was working for Big Brother/Big Sister, I couldn't tell you how many times the parent of a child being mentored told me this: the day the child knew he or she would be meeting with their mentor they would get up early or talk about it all the way to school. I would share it with the mentor, and they would say something like, "Wow, all we do is shoot hoops, or read or talk or go for a walk." When we think about giving, our minds often go to helping the poor, but just as important is the giving of our time.

Gavin D. Becker in his book, *The Gift of Fear*, tells a story about meeting with some men in jail and sharing the sad story of his own childhood. One man asked him, "How come you are on the other side of the table wearing a suit and free to come and go as you please, and we are locked up in here when we all have the same sad story?" His answer was, "Someone believed in me." He says that having a mentor, just one person, or being in a program like Big Brother/Big Sister can make all the difference in a child's life. You could be that person by offering them the gift of time. When you give the gift of time, the goal is not necessarily that the person will be changed, but in the context of relationship, we believe, love, encourage, and hope for another.

Becoming a Mentor: Questions and Thoughts

Mentoring is as old as the world and is one of our greatest commodities.When mentors first start with Big Brother/ Big Sister, they ask if they can buy gifts for the kids. I tell them not to start with stuff; start with you. Send the message that you believe there is no substitute for relationship. Like the Beatles always said - money can't buy love. Don't try to fill their emptiness with transitory things like toys, junk food, or ice cream. Fill their cups with you first.

Ideas for Younger Mentors:

Get involved in the Big Brother/Big Sister Program or some similar program by tutoring, reading, and/or working with younger kids. Some communities have a school program so high school students can be mentors. Someone in Kansas City started a program for adults to go into inner-city elementary schools to read to, and listen to the reading of, fourth grade children. One little girl said her weekly mentoring time was the only time she had a conversation with an adult and heard the English language spoken during the week other than her teacher! It is so easy to get involved. It only takes about an hour a week, and the kids not only love it! They are learning to love to read, an important foundation to a good education and a better future. The program, Lead to Read, is in its second year and has expanded to more schools with dozens of adult volunteers. Could you do something like that in your community?

Mentor Someone Much Older than You:

Consider a reverse mentorship. Look for adults that have challenges with technology or some other area you know something about. Think of what you have to offer an elderly person: going for a stroll, playing a board game, helping with a cell phone or computer. Once you get to know them, you will hear good stories about events that happened before you were born--the privilege of hearing history first-hand. The gift of time and talent from a younger person could mean the world to someone who has lapsed into isolation because they think the world has passed them by.

"Never underestimate the power of mentoring."

My kids and I took care of a man with Alzheimer's disease. We would take him along with us for our morning errands. He would say things like, "Hey, there is the house we used to live in, remember that? Remember when we lived there? " I had instructed my kids to go along with it and have fun. When it is an illness like

Alzheimer's, going along isn't lying; it is allowing a way for the one suffering to live. It is making his or her life more bearable.

So the kids would agree, and then he would throw in something else, and they would throw in some imaginary things and we would laugh and have fun. His wife would tell me she thought he was getting better because he had so much fun with us. Other caretakers might correct him and would tell him no and frustrate him. But what is the point of that? We entered his world and helped him feel he had his bearings.

Would you call this a mentoring situation? Maybe not for our friend with Alzheimer's, but certainly for my children. They learned a great deal from him, and later in life when they came into the working world it served them. They have all run into situations where they realized the person they were dealing with wasn't "all there." They never took it personally, and they knew how to affirm the humanity of the other person in the situation.

Were they mentored by a man with Alzheimer's? I think so. I am so glad we had the opportunity to hang out with Bob. My kids and I will never forget him.

No matter what your age, find someone to mentor, hang out with, and find some one to mentor you. I know it can be hard to find someone in that capacity, as it was for me. Don't give up. Find someone doing what you want to do and ask if you can tag along. Ask questions. If you love working on cars, find a mechanic who doesn't mind you tagging along. If you love art, find an artist and see if you can spend time in her or his workshop. Look for what you love. If you love horses, find someone with horses, or a stable; offer to help them so you can learn from them. See those connections and friendships as mentoring experiences.

"...it can be hard to find someone in that capacity, as it was for me. Don't give up."

The reason I like to address young people with this idea is that while I worked with Big Brother/Big Sister, the teens willing to mentor the elementary school kids were very confident. They believed they had something to offer because all the "Littles" thought it was amazing to hang out with someone actually in high school. All they had to do was show up and the Little was impressed. I rarely had to convince the teens they had something to offer. The adults were a different story. They needed loads of encouragement. If the adult Bigs weren't getting a thank you from the Little, they would sometimes get worried that they weren't doing their jobs. Many adults wondered if they were making a difference at all.

What I learned is that many of these children feared abandonment. They wondered if the adult would get tired of them and go away. When the child didn't seem excited to see them, the adult Big would worry that the Little didn't like them.

The reality was that there were many other things in play. Adults worry more and don't trust themselves as much as the teens, but the worst thing they could do is throw in the towel, because the Littles need to see that there are adults in this world who won't give up on them.

The animated movie UP is a beautiful story of mentorship, and doing life together. The old guy is plagued by a boy scout who "wants to help" and the little scout ends up going on an incredible adventure with the grumpy old man. It is reverse mentoring in its truest form. We really do need each other and some times a little persistence goes a long way.

Many of the high school students who signed up to mentor the younger kids let me know that they loved the experience so much that they are continuing to mentor. The kids who benefited from being mentored or mentoring at an early age, are more likely to become mentors as adults. So, are we adult mentors making a difference? You bet. Real change is slow but sure.

When my kids were young, I would seek out other single moms to spend time with them at the park or somewhere our kids could play and we could talk. I didn't offer much advice, but I was a good listener. I asked what was working for them. I ended up getting so much from the relationships, like great, easy recipes, fun stories, validation, and friendship. Mentoring will take different forms during different times of your life. Don't wait until you are older and wiser. Reach out now. Mentor and be mentored.

WARNING TO POTENTIAL MENTORS: YOU DO NOT HAVE TO HAVE YOUR LIFE NICE AND TIDY IN ORDER TO OFFER YOUR GIFTS TO OTHERS. GOOD MENTORS OFFER WHO THEY ARE NOT WHAT THEY THINK THEY NEED TO BE.

Be a Mentor

If you're doing what you love, there is no greater gift than to help someone else who wants to do something similar. It's the "pay it forward" idea. Take someone under your wing.

In fact, if you know a single parent, reach out to her kids, find a way to connect with them and spend time. Don't try to "teach;" just be a friend. Help them with a project, chores, and building things. Find a way to give some of your time to a kid who doesn't have the benefit of two parents. Or maybe you know a family with a child who has special needs and the other child is getting passed up. Can you spend time with them? Give and be willing to receive. Give what you know from who you are.

"Don't try to "teach;" just be a friend."

I do a little workshop called "The Art of Asking Questions." It's about being curious. It is a great tool for mentoring and life in general. I have learned the importance of asking questions rather than assuming answers. I have come to realize people don't think it is polite to ask questions or be curious. But I encourage you to be curious, to ask questions. We all want someone to listen to us and get to know us. That is the result of being curious and learning the art of asking the questions.

"I have come to realize people don't think it is polite to ask questions or be curious."

Just Wondering:

How are you at asking questions?

What is one question you have asked someone today?

What does it mean to you to be curious?

What has it been like for you to have someone really interested in finding out about you by asking questions and being curious?

How can you incorporate asking questions into your daily life, job, friendships, or family?

When have you been mentored? Believed in? Encouraged?

How can you turn that around and offer it back?

What does mentoring mean to you?

What do you have to offer?

What simple thing can you do that you can share with someone else? Sing, draw, sew?

Make a list of things you do that seem so simple you take for granted. Look at the list. With a willingness to share your gifts of time and talent, you may discover opportunities all around you. Mentoring doesn't have a time limit or age limit. If you are twelve you can mentor someone younger, Start now so you will be in good practice for your twilight years.

Who is one person you can reach out to this week or this month?

If you do not have a mentor, look for someone who is doing something you want to learn. Ask them if they are willing to teach you. Who comes to your mind?

What may prevent you from asking for his or her help?

What relationship are you in now that could be considered a mentoring situation? What is it like for you?

Is there someone you would like to reach out to but are not sure how? How do you envision reaching out?

Sometimes when I asked someone to "mentor" me it would scare them away. Phrases like "Could we have coffee?" "Can I go with you?" and "I will take you," offer a chance to be with them, but takes away the pressure.

What do you have to offer someone?

What would you like to learn from someone else?

Look at the list of what you love. Is there something you would like to learn?

Rock tumbling?

Beach combing?

Thrift shopping?

Bird watching?

Horseback riding?

Gardening?

Cooking/Baking?

Anything you want to learn, you can find a class or a person who is doing it to learn from.

I dare you.

Reach out.

Find a mentor.

Be a Mentor.

18

Balancing Life: Real or Myth

"The journey is finding balance.
The myth is perfect balance."

--Laurie Ann Hardie

How do we devote the proper time to each of the important areas I have described in this book? How does one develop healthy relationships with God, family, and friends? How do we find time for all the things that nourish our lives and our minds: eating well, caring for our bodies, investing for our financial security, giving generously of money and time, feeding our minds and spirits, earning our daily bread, volunteering for worthy causes, and mentoring others for enriching lives?

Finding balance is very difficult for single parents, especially. Rightly or wrongly, being a "single parent" implies something is missing: inherent imbalance. You are doing family on your own. There are so many areas of life, and balancing them all takes a lot of effort, perhaps effort and time we feel we don't have.

When I look back on my life as a single parent and consider all the areas of my life, I get the feeling of imbalance. I spent the bulk of my time with my kids, and at work to support us. Survival left just about no time for friends or self-care. It seems we barely got by.

There was always something new that came along that required money: School clothes, classroom supplies, school fees, sports equipment, social activities, honor banquets, and the list goes on. My life wasn't what anyone would deem balanced. The balanced life I longed for felt like a luxury that could never be obtained.

"Finding balance is very difficult for single parents,... The balanced life I longed for felt like a luxury that could never be obtained."

I dreamed of having time with friends, and I wanted to be able to do some fun things, if only to get my mind off the daily struggles. I found free things to do, but I really missed going with my friends to a movie, dinner, and just hanging out. I had to be home when I wasn't working, giving rides, making meals, helping with homework, waiting to pick up or drop off one child or the other. It seemed like I was trapped.

I couldn't work any harder to make more money because then I would have no time with my kids. I wasn't eating healthy because the inexpensive food we ate was often high in fat, sugar, and calories. I would love to be able to tell you that I found a way to balance it all, something that you could bank on, and that could inspire you who find yourselves in the same situations. Sadly, that's just not the case.

I didn't have much time for me, and thus balance was an elusive dream. I felt like Erich Brenn, that guy who had a plate-spinning act on the old television variety shows. My spinning plates were the kids, my job, friendships, and education. I ran from area to area and would spin plates on top of spindles. After the last plate was set spinning nicely, the first plate began to wobble and I would have to set it in motion once again.

Truth be told, my plates always wobbled! It wasn't pretty, but there was just enough balance to keep me in the game of life.

Then there were the earth-bound plates that neither spun nor wobbled: the things in my life that felt too overwhelming to deal with. I had cars (plural) in my yard that were not running. Should I have them hauled away or hope they could be fixed? Every time I left the house or drove up after work there it was: Laurie's Salvage. Sheet metal stressors - what was I to do? Finally, I called the recycle center and asked them to come and take them away.

It was really hard for me to let go of one of these vehicles. It was a huge old gas-hogging Chevy Suburban with so many cherished family memories attached to it. I couldn't afford to fix it or feed it. So when the man from the recycling center came to take it away, I was sad. I may have cried. But once it was gone, so was the daily anxiety of seeing it the yard. Only when it was gone, did I realize what an emotional drain an object could be.

"These items were a reflection of the emotional clutter going on within me."

Single parents are often attached to memories, and there is a grief of letting go of something that is a reminder of good memories. It's hard to admit that an old standby is now causing stress, rather than creating good thoughts.

Maybe you need the help of someone to give perspective and understanding as you part with treasured items. I couldn't have parted with these albatrosses without the help of my friends. They would often help me take the difficult step to create space for myself.

These items were a reflection of the emotional clutter going on within me. I had to break it down to the simplest terms. Dealing with what was taking up space freed me to no longer carry the emotional baggage that went along with it. I needed to claim space so that my family and I could have some peace.

What are you putting up with that is draining your time and energy? Could it be unfinished projects hanging over your head? Broken everyday things in your home? A broken-down car? Outmoded furniture or appliances that are taking up too much space? Overdue paperwork?

Make your list and prioritize by the easiest to the hardest. What can you do to get the stresses off your list? Keep it and use it? Get rid of it? Give it away? What is one step you can do today toward making space for you?

Once the albatross is gone or the project is completed, how do you feel? Celebrate the fact that you finished it, even if it was just making a necessary phone call! Whoop it up a little! Now that you have eliminated one small thing, how good is it going to feel to take care of the next small thing? Eventually you will make it to the big things.

"I had a hard time giving up unfinished projects."

I had a hard time giving up unfinished projects. There were projects I knew I wouldn't find the time to finish, and I had to give myself permission to pass them on, throw them away, or give them to the thrift store. What permission can you grant yourself?

Sometimes misinformation feeds our dread in dealing with things. For example, I thought I would have to pay to get rid of the cars so I put it off. I took one step and made a call and found out that paying wasn't the issue. Guilt set in for a few moments, because I felt like I should sell them and get some money, but on further reflection, I realized I didn't have the time to deal with that. So I gave myself permission to just let them go. Now that the stress was gone, I was able to focus on more important things.

"We forget the things that make the memories that sustain us through the inevitable storms ahead."

Oh, to have some balance! In the midst of raising kids, family meant everything. It took most of my time and energy. It was what I worked hard at and what mattered the most to me. Now as an empty nester, family still matters to me, but my grown kids are the busy ones now. They don't have me to cook, drive, or arrange things for them. I am not helping with homework and projects. I am not going to after-school dances or football games.

Now my life has a different balance, so to speak, with family. Work now takes more of my time and energy. Perfect balance isn't the answer, but some sort of balance at each phase of our lives is helpful. It's so easy to get so caught up in what we think is important and urgent (but which often isn't) that we forget to have some fun, take a rest, or do something frivolous. We forget the things that make the memories that sustain us through the inevitable storms ahead.

In the midst of the struggle to survive with the plate-spinning of life, our perception of balance must take a back seat to what we truly need for our soul's nourishment. Make time to savor the small moments, take a mini-vacation, escape to an inspiring place, observe your giggling children at the zoo, and breathe in the wonder of everyday life. You will find perspective. You will also discover that taking a break doesn't do much to even out the scales of your life, but it sure seems to keep the heavy stuff from breaking us.

Just Wondering:

What are you tolerating?

What excuses keep you from making changes in what you are tolerating?

What would your life be like if just one of the things you're tolerating was gone?

How would that feel?

What will it take to move in the direction of dealing with just one of the issues? What is one small step you can take?

Just one thing on the list. Just one step towards eliminating it from your stressors. I dare you to eliminate one thing. Then celebrate; it will no longer suck the life out of you. Now just one more.

19

A Final Note, I did not see that coming.

I hope there have been some things in this book that have given you hope or validated you. Single parenting isn't easy at its best. It demands so much of our time, energy, creativity and strength. It is a blessed thing to be a parent and have the responsibility of raising good citizens. It's what we hope for, but life gets in the way. Kids have disabilities and disorders. Life doesn't go as we planned. There are struggles and victories, good times and bad.

"I wanted a pat on the back, not a kick in the butt."

There are times when, as hard as we try to be part of a community, we find ourselves all alone. It feels like we're climbing uphill with a broken leg trying to carry a boulder. It seems impossible. Those are the times you find the courage to remind yourself you are not alone, and you will make it. Those were the hardest times for me. I wanted to sink into despair and self-pity. I wanted someone to say, "How in the world are you making it?" I wanted a pat on the back, not a kick in the butt.

But these are the times I cannot allow myself the indulgence of self-pity. These are the times I tell myself, "Don't go there." There are times when I have to pick myself up when I feel like going to bed and never rising again. My lifeline has been my faith in a God who is much bigger than I. He encourages me never to give up and gives me strength to take the next step.

My faith reminds me that I can't do it all or be it all. It reminds me that even though I feel like I'm not enough, I can offer what I have. So there will be times when the school lunches you fix are boring, and maybe you can't afford school pictures, or new shoes. Rather than living a tragedy, you can make it an adventure. Your children will look to you to set the tone.

"My faith has taught me the power of gratitude."

Perhaps you'll find you're at your wit's end and you heave some old mugs at a brick wall or smash 'em with a hammer. It does feel kind of good.Expect bad days and celebrate the good ones.

Let your friends and family help you, and let others into your life, even though it maybe messy and chaotic. Remember they won't say things perfectly and they will give unasked-for advice, but they will mean you well more than they will wish you ill.

My faith has taught me the power of gratitude. When we struggle, it's easy to focus on what we don't have and who's not there. One day, when I felt like I had nothing, a friend encouraged me to open my cupboards. I saw what I had and was able to feel thankful. Encouragement can come from surprising places, and often where and when we least expect it.

Some people will be there for you for just one time. It may be tempting to focus on how they dropped the ball, rather than being grateful for what they offered to you. Turn your resentment of people into gratitude to God for what He has provided, both big and small.

There are things I had to learn to live with and to live without. God is my provider and He does not work from my to-do or must-have list. Gratitude is not for things; it is for a relationship that will never leave. Gratitude lifts me from being another victim of my circumstances to being a person who believes I am truly loved.

My faith encourages me to never give up, to really believe whatever is overwhelming...that this too shall pass. I am here to tell you that it will not always be like it is right now.

Dreams are a part of hope and the belief in a better day. I believed when to do so seemed ridiculous. My dreams brought hope. They brought something to make me wonder about and be curious. It is not only good for us to dream, but also good for our families. It communicates that there is something beyond difficult circumstances. Our children need to see us put the oxygen mask on ourselves, just like in the airplane flight instructions.

"Take time to breathe, to get your bearings, and remind yourself about who you really are."

Take time to breathe, to get your bearings, and remind yourself about who you really are. Remember who you are is not just a taxi driver, bed tucker-in-er, storyteller, lunch deliver-er, cheerleader, disciplinarian, cook, housekeeper, tear wiper, and mama bear. You are fully loved, and you are a beautiful being who was created to dream.

If I can leave you with my wish, it is never to give up, never to stop pursuing your purpose, never to settle for "Sorry, this is as good as it gets."

Be a receiver

Live don't just survive

Believe

Be disappointed

Hope

Wonder

Experience the Journey

There is light at the end of the tunnel and it isn't a train.

Just Wondering:

What will you take away from this book?

Were you challenged? If so, write about it in your journal, or have a conversation about it with a friend.

Were you encouraged? If so, write about it in your journal, or talk with a friend about it.

About the author...

Laurie Hardie is a genius at making something out of nothing.

She has a BA in Social Services, is a Certified Life Coach and Spiritual Director, and has 30 years of experience in broadcasting. Along her journey, she's had to call on every single one of those skills to survive. When life throws rocks, she builds castles.

Laurie raised three children and 89,542 animals on an island in the Pacific Northwest. After coming out of the closet while the kids were young, her husband took all of her best clothes - and cemented her status as Single Mom.

This is when Laurie learned first-hand what it means to live in community. While working for Big Brother/ Big Sister and other volunteer organizations, she developed her skills as a gardener, crafter, seamstress, writer, and speaker.

A noted author, speaker, and broadcast personality, Laurie now resides in the Pacific Northwest.

Laurie's message to you...

Even if you think your life is over, it isn't!

"Where you are" means where you are NOW and it can change. It doesn't have to be the end; it can be the starting point for something new.

Look, it really is okay to struggle sometimes. It's also okay to allow other people to help. If you're having a hard time, that doesn't mean you have nothing to contribute! Even if you don't believe it yet, you do have something valuable and precious to offer. We can give out of our nothingness - out of our despair - out of our loneliness, even if it seems the whole world is against you...even if it seems God has forgotten you, there's hope for you, too.

That dream you have? It can still come to you, although it may change form. You don't have to be able to see the whole way right now. There are baby steps you can take every day to bring that dream closer to reality.

Bottom line - this is a message of hope and healing for single parents. If you're struggling and alone right now, there is hope for you. If your church or community doesn't understand, know that there is still a place for you somewhere. If you know someone who's scrambling to hold it all together, there are some real-world things you can do to help.

Live what you love,

~Laurie Hardie

About Coaching...

Coaching is a partnership to support you in your journey. A coach will encourage you and hold you accountable. With a coach, it's easier to accomplish things you never thought possible. A coach believes in you and helps you discover and use your strengths. Coaching is about you and for you.

Coaching changed my life and it can change yours as well. Don't let money get in the way. There are people and organizations that will sponsor single moms to get coaching. Sometimes it takes asking for the help. But it is so worth the effort.

If you're interested in a free consult, contact me at lacoach@ comcast.net

To your dreams,
Coach Laurie

About Speaking...

If you would like to have Laurie speak at your event, contact her at lacoach@comcast.net.

Topics include:

Single Parenting

Hope

Encouragement

Living what you love

Leadership

Mentoring

Personal Growth

Sudden Chaos

Her talks are entertaining, informative and real.

For a demo, go to DidNotSeeThatComing.com or CoachLaurie.com and click the speaking tab.